MASTER THE MATRIX

7 ESSENTIALS FOR GETTING THINGS DONE IN COMPLEX ORGANIZATIONS

D1004598

MASTER THE MATRIX

7 ESSENTIALS FOR GETTING THINGS DONE IN COMPLEX ORGANIZATIONS

SUSAN Z. FINERTY

Two Harbors Press
212 3rd Avenue North, Suite 290
Minneapolis, MN 55401
612.455.2293
www.TwoHarborsPress.com

ISBN-13: 978-1-937293-98-7
LCCN: 2011944167

Distributed by Itasca Books

Printed in the United States of America

For my Mom, Jeanine Bentley Zelmanski (1937-1998):
Not exactly what you imagined (kind of like me).

CONTENTS

FOREWORD

During my 23-year career at Baxter International, I often encouraged our team members to "manage the intersections!" We were a global, multi-divisional corporation, and there were plenty of intersections—global goals intersecting with local needs, functional initiatives intersecting with business decisions. I knew that this thing we called "the matrix" wasn't going away. I truly believed that we needed to find a way to use lthe matrix to optimize the entire organization, versus trying to optimize each part individually.

Not only was "the matrix" not going away, figuring out how to leverage it became our competitive advantage. Managing the often unclear and ambiguous matrix is a capability so uncommon that mastering it can be the difference between a good company and a truly outstanding one.

But mastering the matrix isn't just an organization's competitive advantage. It is your competitive advantage. That's difficult to see, and we may find ourselves complaining or wishing it away. The key is to take a big step back, get your arms around the entire organization and make it work for you. That requires you to really get to know the organization, understand the intersections and view the management of those intersections as a key part of your role. The people who do this not only succeed but, even more importantly, get a lot more satisfaction out of what they do.

What Susan does in this book is provide you with the tools to make the matrix work—from how to build partnerships that ease goal alignment, role clarity and decision-making to the key skills of influence, communication and meeting facilitation that enable you to gain traction and accomplish things in a matrix role. And getting things done is really what it's all about. At the end of the day—have you made a difference? Have you moved the organization forward? Do you feel a sense of pride and accomplishment in your work?

Susan also provides us a framework for discussing and assessing what it really means to "manage the intersections." With the tools in this book, when we run up against a barrier, we can diagnose it and work to resolve it.

Organizations are becoming more complex and so are our roles. Your tendency may be to try to avoid or ignore the matrix, simplify or narrow your scope, working only within the confines of your role or team. When you are tempted to do this, reach for this book. Mastering the matrix—not oversimplifying it, discounting it or hoping it goes away—is the key to your success...enjoy your journey.

HARRY M. JANSEN KRAEMER, JR.
Author, From Values to Action: The Four Principles of Values-Based Leadership
Professor, Northwestern University's Kellogg School of Management
Former Chairman and CEO, Baxter International

Unfortunately, no one can be
told what the Matrix is.
You have to see it for yourself.

WELCOME TO THE MATRIX
A TALE OF TWO PARTNERS

FOR Nancy, it truly was the best of times and the worst of times. In describing the wealth of corporate resources she needed to work through to get her job done, Nancy stated bluntly, "There was one relationship in this corporate maze that really worked, one that was a complete roadblock and the rest were various shades of roadblock."

Nancy was in a matrix role, specifically what I call a Customer Hub Matrix. She was an HR person who relied on various centralized, corporate shared-service organizations to bring services and products to her internal customers. Nancy supported Manufacturing, which was not only geographically remote, but seemingly a world away from the culture at corporate headquarters. An idea that made perfect sense for 4,000 people at Corporate in suburban LA made no sense whatsoever to a plant of 600 in rural Mississippi. Nancy was a traffic cop at the intersection of local needs and corporate goals.

She had five different corporate areas in her hub. Two of these provide a great illustration of the good and bad of matrix relationships. Sharon was Nancy's partner for delivering Employee Benefits to her internal customers. Fran was her partner for delivering HR information systems. The two partnerships could not have been more different.

Fran headed a group that was responsible for all HR information systems (HRIT). At the time, Fran and Nancy were both on a team charged with design and installation of new HR and Payroll systems. Nancy also connected with Fran and her team on a daily basis to sort out more routine systems issues and projects. At first, things were smooth, and they had a few accomplishments, both for the corporate team and for the manufacturing plants. But as time went on and the stakes got higher, Nancy grew increasingly frustrated by "how to get them to provide services to my business in a way that meets Manufacturing's needs and expectations…they couldn't customize anything, had really long lead time, they just didn't get it. It was like we were operating in totally different universes."

Any connected tasks were complicated by near-constant perceptions of trespassing onto each other's "turf." Decision-making provided regular controversy over who the decision maker was, what decisions they needed to make together and what decisions they needed to give the other a heads up on. They rarely agreed on tactics, let alone bigger picture goals. It became a classic "throw it over the fence" relationship. HRIT would make a decision or create a solution and pass it over. When Nancy was asked for input on a decision or solution and provided it, she was met with, "We can't do it that way; we aren't going to customize for one group of employees." According to Nancy, "They had one way of doing things, and there was absolutely no flexibility on that. The rules and regulations were black and white, rarely any flexibility."

"As more managers gain experience operating in matrix organizations, they are bound to spread this experience. We believe that in the future matrix organizations managers will speak less of the difficulties and pathologies than of its advantages and benefits."

HARVARD BUSINESS REVIEW, 1978

After several rounds of this, Nancy stopped giving input, and they stopped asking for it. Nancy did the bare basics to implement their work products and jerry-rigged things behind the scenes. The silos were built and reinforced with every interaction. The amount of energy consumed in silo building and the hours consumed in work-arounds were significant. The divide wasn't just between Nancy and Fran, but between individuals on their teams as well. The rift was ongoing and obvious.

Communication became more and more constricted as Nancy and Fran's trust unraveled. Doling out answers to only the questions that were asked, sharing only what was absolutely necessary. Nancy described meetings as "one pack against another." At one point, a meeting that was supposed to include a total of five people representing both teams grew to 10+. There was standing room only, both teams congregating on their side of the room. Given the nature of the discussion in the meeting, it was an apparent attempt to overrule by outnumbering—on both sides.

After relaying this story to me, Nancy paused and said, "It's actually my big regret—that I didn't try harder or try a different way to make that relationship work. Surely there was something I could have done?"

She then proceeded to tell me about Sharon. Sharon was on the opposite end of the partnership spectrum. When Sharon joined the company, Nancy saw an opportunity for a fresh start with a person who she would need to work closely with. Sharon's predecessor was a reasonable partner, but in Sharon, Nancy saw the chance to form an even stronger collaboration.

She started by initiating a visit to Sharon at corporate headquarters. Then she took Sharon to a couple of plants so she could get a feel for the manufacturing culture and realities. Determined to make this work, Nancy included Sharon and her team in her meetings, readily and routinely shared information and brought them in on planning and decision-making. At first Sharon's reciprocation was scant, but it grew over time as Nancy persisted.

As I interviewed leaders for this book, I could tell the complexity of their matrix by the number of words it took to explain it.

The record?
462 words.

The partnership grew and sustained even through a few crises. "It was just so easy—there were none of the extra-curricular issues to deal with like there were with Fran and her team. It was smooth, even when times were rough." Nancy found herself far less frustrated by the fact that corporate couldn't always give her what she needed—she was willing to give and take, choose her battles. Even when decisions and solutions didn't meet 100% of Manufacturing's needs, Nancy and her team worked to implement them.

Nancy's relationship with Sharon spread to her team and her customers. Sharon's team enjoyed a unique place in the heart of the manufacturing team— the corporate team that really "gets it." In Nancy's words, "Once I had built the relationship, whether my expectations changed of what they could provide, or they provided better service, it just went a lot better. I could understand what they could really give me, where they had flexibility and where they didn't, and they understood the same from me and my business."

There are many reasons for the differences between these two partnerships—experiences and styles of the people involved, nature of the projects, even timing. These variables are not replicable, and while they might make an interesting read, the application is limited. But within this story also lie principles and practices that make matrix roles work. The partnerships that were formed, goals that were aligned (or misaligned), clarity of roles, communication and influence practices that were utilized apply in all sorts of matrix situations. So in answer to Nancy's question of whether she could have done things differently with Fran, the answer is yes. These techniques were identified in my surveys and interviews of over 100 experienced matrix managers and form the backbone of this book.

The other thing that carries over from this story is the complexity of the backdrop. The maze of people and cross-functional teams that Nancy worked through is typical of large corporations everywhere. Traditional structures and roles in which titles are descriptors of how work gets done are gone. They have been replaced by organizational mazes that are rarely self-explanatory.

HOW DID THINGS GET SO COMPLICATED?

"Matrix" organization structures first came into vogue in the 1960s as a way to organize around key projects in the burgeoning aerospace industry. Through the 70s and 80s, commercial industry picked up on the trend with mixed success. Organizational design researchers Larson and Gobeli (1987) provide a workable definition of a traditional matrix organization:

> "A 'mixed' organizational form in which normal hierarchy is 'overlaid' by some form of lateral authority, influence or communication...there are usually two chains of command, one along functional lines and the other along project lines."

Much has been written of project managers who sit at the crossroads between reporting through the project management structure and through their "business" boss as described above. *But the matrix isn't just for project managers anymore.* Informal matrices and matrixed teams are cropping up in organizations that don't call themselves "matrix organizations." This once formally named and managed structure has morphed into overlapping organizational webs that are often navigated with little or no guidance.

These webs are sprouting up as the traditional business structure of multiple, independently operated business units shifts to shared services, cross-functional teams and "flatter" organizations. All these efforts are aimed at doing more with less and gaining "economies of scale," and they all create matrices.

In addition, automation, globalization, regulation and legislation have created a reality in which few tasks, projects or goals fall neatly into one person or team's bailiwick. Instead they cut across teams, functions and geographies.

Problems stretch across multiple organizational territories, as do their solutions and the processes for reaching them. To manage these tasks and solve these problems, organizations began to form around them, formally and informally—through full-on teams or individual reporting relationships. These matrix structures are intended to maximize the power of intersections—intersections between global businesses and local resources, between technical expertise and business units and among multiple functions. Nancy, in the opening story, found herself at the dead center of a matrix between corporate shared services and her manufacturing internal customers.

There is undoubtedly power to be had at these intersections—tough, complex problems can be solved and multi-pronged strategies carried out here. But they can feel more like labyrinths than intersections to those attempting to navigate them.

WHY PEOPLE WORKING IN MATRIX ROLES DESPERATELY NEED A BOOK ABOUT IT

Matrix roles (and the challenges and frustrations that go with them) are everywhere. The field customer contact person who has to work through a maze of resources to write contracts, negotiate delivery and troubleshoot product issues. The product manager in Singapore who is simultaneously accountable for numbers in her country, region and business unit despite the fact they are in conflict. The HR person who reports to a globalized HR function, with a dotted line to the head of the business he/she supports. All of these are matrix roles.

"The biggest mistake people make in matrix situations? Assuming they can't do anything about it."

EXECUTIVE COACH

When the matrix practitioners I connected with described their matrix roles they used words like confusing, chaotic, convoluted and frustrating. Operating in a web of authority, on multiple dimensions and sometimes at cross-purposes can be draining to even the most energetic matrix managers.

The matrix turns our traditional assumptions about hierarchy, power and authority upside down, blurring lines of authority that were once crystal clear. Job titles no longer bring with them everything needed to get the results that we are held accountable for. "Decision-maker" distinctions that used to be illustrated by title and office size are disappearing. Pinpointing who is in the catbird seat becomes less and less clear, and multiple customer groups with disparate needs tapping into the same pool of resources drown out the traditional cry of "the customer is always right."

You are probably nodding your head in agreement to the realities listed above. Getting results in matrix roles is as different from traditional roles as basketball is from swimming. Different rules apply; different skills are needed. But when we are in the middle of these matrix intersections, we often try to apply the same traditional approaches to getting things done. It's like trying to dribble a basketball in four feet of water.

Matrix mastery is becoming a distinguishing competency at every level of organizations. The skills clustered around matrix management represent the very definition of what it means to lead in modern organizations. Attempts to job-hop yourself away from matrix roles are a wasted effort. You have to hone your proficiency and make your skills and practices portable—corporate reorgs, mergers, acquisitions and job changes all require you to pick up and establish yourself anew as a matrix manager. This book will be a resource for you in current and future matrix roles.

There are ways to gain traction and be successful in these roles. It's not "just the way it is." There are specific skills and practices you can apply to get things done. Through surveys and interviews, experienced matrix practitioners weigh in on these in the chapters that follow.

IT'S NOT ABOUT THE BOXES

Researchers and authors have done considerable work examining the optimal dimensions of a matrix, structure and strategy alignment, how to implement a matrix structure, etc. Organizations frequently look to reshuffle the deck and consider how they can reorganize the matrix for better results.

The architecture of matrix structures is important—like a house built on a faulty foundation, no amount of individual skill or diligence will keep an illogical, nonsensical structure standing. But the fact is, although matrix structures start as boxes on paper, they rely on people to work. Where this book picks up is what happens *after the boxes are laid out.* It's about the partnerships, the end game of these partnerships and the skills that get you there.

WHAT TYPE OF MATRIX ROLE ARE YOU IN?

Matrix roles are set up to enable organizations to get the best of both worlds. An organization wants global oversight and local autonomy so they set up a dotted line reporting relationship across geographies, connecting the goals of the global corporation and the local team. They want to support business units without recreating support teams all over the company, so shared service teams are created, bringing the competing priorities and goals of business units to the desks of the team members. To ensure that product design teams stay connected with the business and the customer, team members report to the Project Lead and to their business. To solve a problem that cuts across multiple functions with a solution that cuts across those same functions, they form cross-functional teams.

Let's get specific about your matrix role. Matrix roles can be seen above you (multiple bosses) and surrounding you (multiple, disparate stakeholders you depend on). Some of the most common matrixed roles are:

Formal project matrix: This is the most "traditional" and established form of matrix. It is defined as having a project management office structure and a functional or business reporting structure. These roles are very common for long-term projects like product development. People are generally 100% allocated to these projects/positions. The idea behind this is to establish dedicated resources that utilize structured project management, but are still held accountable to the function or business that owns the final product.

> *"I am an engineer on a product development project. On the 'official' org chart, I report to the Engineering Department Head. In reality I spend 80% of my time and get 80% of my work and direction from the project manager for a development team I am a part of—she's my 'dotted line' boss."*

Cross-functional team matrix: These have cropped up all over organizations as a way to solve problems and keep the business moving. They are generally for specific (and often short-term) projects/issues. The idea behind this type of matrix is that more minds = better problem identification and better solutions.

> *"I am the head of a commercialization team for a product launch in Europe. My job is to design and execute a launch strategy that all country teams buy into."*

Reporting relationship matrix: This is most often seen as an outgrowth of globalization. Often, globalization includes centers of expertise that maximize the knowledge of specialists and maintain local offices to maximize proximity to customers and markets. So while a person (say

HR, Marketing, Finance) may report to a centralized head of their function or region, he or she may also have a solid or dotted line to a business or geography. This dual-reporting relationship is intended to ensure that the specialist doesn't operate in a vacuum, removed from those whom he/she supports.

> *"My boss is the VP of HR for Spain, but I work with the head of the business on a daily basis and also need to make sure that I am doing what the corporate HR team expects."*

Customer "hub" matrix: Companies often have dedicated customer teams whose sole purpose is to work together to meet the needs of specific internal and external customers. More and more, these teams are not fully dedicated to one customer or even customer group. Instead they are a "shared service" that supports a line of products or even an entire business. Nancy in The Tale of Two Partners was in an internal customer hub, but they can be seen with external customers as well. It is left to the customer contact to orchestrate all that is needed to deliver on customer needs.

> *"I am the key customer contact for this territory. My company has six different divisions. My customers order products from all six divisions. Most of my job entails negotiating and executing contracts across these six divisions. I am all matrix—none of these people report to me."*

These four types of matrix roles may differ in how and why they are set up, but they have common challenges and require common underlying skills and practices.

WE KNOW IT WHEN WE SEE IT

It may have been easy to identify which matrix role best describes your own. Plotting a course for success in your role is a little trickier.

In his opinion for Jacobellis v. Ohio in 1964, Supreme Court Justice Potter Stewart said of the French film, *The Lovers*, "hard-core pornography is hard to define, but I know it when I see it … and the motion picture involved in this case is not that."

Matrix management is a little like that—you've probably seen people who navigate matrix roles and organizations well. They persevere where others have given up and flourish where others have faded. But "You either got it, or you don't" isn't exactly helpful if you are trying to improve your matrix management abilities.

If you have ever sought coaching on how to steer your way through a matrix role, chances are you met with blank stares or vague suggestions. Like many skills, people who are masters of the matrix may not be able to explain what they do or why they do it. Even leaders who are great coaches may struggle with helping to develop this one—so don't be surprised if even your highly successful boss isn't conversant on the topic.

That's because we haven't pinpointed what "good" (or preferably "great") looks like. The Seven Essentials that make up this book are a start to naming what it takes to achieve results in matrix roles:

Regardless of which matrix role best describes your current post, this is how you gain traction. The Essentials vary in importance and application based on the type of matrix role you are in, and these variances are outlined at the end of each chapter.

THE BUILDING BLOCKS

There are four common elements, or Building Blocks, woven throughout the book:

MINDSET

JUJITSU

ZOOM OUT

TRIAGE

You will see icons in each chapter that pull out ideas related to these elements in each chapter. They serve as an "at-a-glance" view of key tips and ideas.

MINDSET

Adjust your thinking and you are halfway to becoming a matrix master. In *The Seven Habits of Highly Effective People*, Stephen Covey does a great job of explaining how the way you think about something affects your actions and ultimately outcomes. He calls it the See-Do-Get Model. How you approach or see things will determine what you do, which in turn leads to your outcomes. If you want different outcomes, you need to start by changing how you view your situation—your mindset.

Trying any of the "how tos" that are part of the Essentials before adopting the right mindset will make your efforts disingenuous and limit your outcomes. Matrix roles differ from traditional roles in terms of clear lines of authority and responsibility, and they also require a different kind of thinking. If you are in a matrix role but retain the mindset of a traditional role, you will dramatically limit what you can accomplish because you will unintentionally create political rifts and disenfranchise co-workers. Your relationships will be too limited, your perspective too narrow and your solutions confined, rudimentary and unsophisticated.

JUJITSU

Jujitsu is a 2,500-year-old martial art that relies on redirecting the force of your opponent, thereby using his/her energy, not your own. Jujitsu is pertinent to matrix masters because conflict (though generally not hand-to-hand conflict!) is what matrix roles are set up to bring out. You can view this conflict as a battle and exhaust yourself fighting, or you can choose to *not* fight fire with fire. If you don't compete (for resources, decisions, control, etc.), your opponent can't win. Instead, try stepping away or disarming the conflict by giving concessions. It may seem counter-intuitive and potentially counter to your organization's culture, but it is a powerful approach that leaves your reputation, values and strength intact.

ZOOM OUT

To succeed in a matrix, you must broaden your perspective. Maintaining a narrow, siloed focus on only your small segment of a project or organization will lead to failure. Matrix Masters must be able to see all the pieces of the puzzle at once to figure out whom to involve, communicate with and influence. The traditional perspective of "I focus on this and this only" will only hurt you in a matrix role. Zooming out can be difficult because when we are overwhelmed or confused, our natural human tendency is to pull back and focus on whatever is right in front of us. These blinders may offer temporary relief, but not a sustainable solution.

TRIAGE

Triage is a medical term that refers to the process of efficiently prioritizing patients based on the severity of their condition when resources are insufficient to treat them all immediately. It comes from the French verb *trier*, meaning to separate, sort, sift or select. Sitting at an intersection with a zoom-out mentality, you will see a lot: discussions that need to take place, decisions that need to be made, problems that need to be solved, conflicts that need to be resolved. But seeing them isn't the same as tackling them. To avoid being completely overwhelmed, you have to triage. I have worked with a number of Emergency Room physicians for whom triage is a way of life. Although the stakes are not quite as high in a matrix role, triage is still vital. You are privy to things you wouldn't see in more traditional roles. But you can't take it all on—you have to triage.

CAVEAT EMPTOR

Although this book is focused on the people who make matrix roles work, clearly these roles do not exist in a vacuum. They are part of organizations and are affected by all elements of the organization.

Herein lies my dilemma: I want this book to empower you. I want you to move from "I surrender," to "Bring it on, I can do this." Too often we give up and resort to blaming the matrix for our lack of success. I want to loosen the handcuffs that we often create for ourselves. But let's be clear: *There are times when matrix roles, even when filled by a master of the skills and practices in this book, will not work. There are times when matrix roles are not set up to succeed.*

How do you know if your role is "not set up to succeed"? Consider the 6 Ps (because any business book worth its salt has a good alliteration): Pay, Power and Politics, Process and Policy, and Pedigree.

PAY. Incentive systems in organizations are a powerful pull. If that pull is not lined up with your direction, it is nearly impossible to change course. For example, if your cross-functional team is incentivized to focus on everything but your project, even if you execute the suggestions in this book to the letter, you will not be able to overcome it. If your solid line boss is incentivized to drive results that conflict with those of your dotted line boss, again, you will not be able to find success easily.

POWER AND POLITICS. In some organizations, the culture is such that power is out of balance—business units have the voice and functions have no say, or there are fierce struggles for power between leaders at the top. Decisions may be centralized at the top, where nothing gets done without a title. To work, matrix organizations and roles must have some balance of power (though not necessarily 50/50), and decision-making rights must exist below the top floor. If not, your efforts in a matrix role may be beset by minefields that are difficult to anticipate and recover from and that can reduce risk-taking and initiative to near zero.

PROCESS AND POLICY. When formal processes for sharing information, making decisions or completing tasks are very hierarchical because they require multiple layers of approval, or when centralization causes a bottleneck, matrix roles can break down. Operating in matrix roles requires both individual and organizational flexibility.

PEDIGREE. Some organizations have widely held assumptions over who can influence decisions (which is an indisputable necessity for success in matrix roles). It may be a matter of experience. If you haven't carried the bag—been a sales rep—then you'll never influence the commercial side. If you've never worked in a plant, good luck influencing anyone on the manufacturing side. If you haven't worked in the industry, then your opinion is discounted. It may be where you grew up, organizationally speaking—what business, function, etc. You may eventually hold influence, but it will take an extended period of time.

My advice to you is to look at these caveats and judge them honestly. No organization has perfectly aligned incentives, a complete balance of power or policies and processes in place that support what you need to get done. You can't wait for or expect perfection, but you also can't expect to drive results when organizational barriers are insurmountable.

GETTING THE MOST OUT OF THIS BOOK

My goal for this book is that it becomes a resource that you turn to over and over again, that you bookmark, highlight and cover with post-its (at least for those of you reading the good old-fashioned print version).

Throughout the book, we will circle back to Nancy and The Tale of Two Partnerships, but you will also see other stories and quotes from the 100+ leaders who were part of my research. Although I have changed their names and background information (to protect the innocent and guilty), their messages are loud and clear.

For the skimmers among you, each chapter is summarized with key concepts you need to **embrace** and ideas to **try**. In addition, there is a final word for each of the four types of matrix roles—so you can see what is especially important based on the nature of your matrix role.

Hundreds of tips and ideas are presented here. Some are new, some familiar, some simple reminders. Not all will be your style, and they will have to be adapted to your situation. Some you will read and think, "yeah, I tried that—it didn't work." When you find yourself with that thought, challenge yourself on two accounts: (1) What would it hurt to try it again? (2) The last time you tried it, did you have the right mindset? As I mentioned previously, trying tips without the right mindset will limit your results.

As with any resource, the real value is your personal commitment to trying things out and taking a risk. These tips may not work the first time, or you may feel clumsy. Give yourself a break and give others a break—it may take them some time to adjust to your new behaviors.

> *"Meet them halfway with love,*
> *peace and persuasion, and expect*
> *them to rise for the occasion."*
>
> VAN MORRISON

ESSENTIAL #1
START WITH PARTNERSHIPS

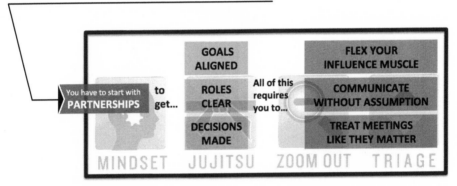

WHAT IT IS

Partnerships are integral to matrix roles, where almost no endeavor is purely independent. The most important skill a matrix practitioner possesses is his or her ability to build, maintain and repair partnerships. These partnerships facilitate goal alignment, role clarity and decision-making, which are the foundation of effective matrix management.

WHAT YOU WILL LEARN

» Who should you be partnering with?
» The Matrix–Partner Continuum™: four types of matrix partnerships
» The partnership mindset: don't wait for them
» Making shifts: five baseline investments
» Compounding your investment
» Pulling back: when your partnership overreaches

"Once I had built the relationship, whether my expectations of what they could provide changed, or they just provided better service, it just went a lot better. I could understand what they could really provide and where they had flexibility and where they didn't, and they understood the same from me and my business."

THE last line from The Tale of Two Partners in the Introduction says it all. Matrix mastery—in all types of matrix roles—starts with partnerships like the one between Nancy and Sharon. But realistically, you don't always have the luxury of building from the ground up. You also have to get good at bringing partnerships back from the brink of disaster. This chapter is the longest and perhaps the most complex in the book, because partnerships themselves are so complex. Mastering the 'who, what and how' of partnerships is critical to getting the most out of the other essentials.

In a matrix role, you are one puzzle piece that fits in with multiple other pieces that you can't always see or understand. Tasks that fall entirely under your control are rare. You are always pulling in others' expertise, approval, arms and legs for implementation. You are absolutely dependent on others to accomplish your goals. That's probably why 95% of survey respondents noted building relationships and the trust they are predicated on as the #1 and #2 most important skills a matrix manager can have.

> 95% of survey respondents noted building relationships and the trust they are predicated on as the #1 and #2 most important skills a matrix manager can have.
>
> **SURVEY** ✓

Partnerships are the grease that makes this interdependence run smoothly. Partnerships allow work to flow unencumbered by suspicion, politics and micro-management. Partnerships actually take work out of the system. Think of all the extra steps you take in checking, following up and verifying when a partnership is lacking. Without strong partnerships, aligning goals takes much longer, roles need to be unrealistically defined and clarified, influence is nearly impossible and decision-making grinds to a halt. We try to make up for deficient partnerships with contracts, covenants, governance, process and policy only to have relationships crushed under the weight of bureaucracy.

Partners take you at face value, even in ambiguous or ill-defined situations. They assume your best intent immediately and are ready to listen and be influenced. They are less stringent with paying back a favor in kind. Their trust can facilitate trust and influence with others, so your impact grows exponentially.

Matrix roles are set up to create conflict—which can fly in the face of partnerships. They bring together a variety of expertise and goals in the hope of finding a solution that provides the best of both worlds. Dotted lines call loyalty into question. Teams and hubs bring together many differences—goals, bosses, geographies. This inherent conflict creates tension that makes building and sustaining partnerships difficult.

Matrix roles force you to be acutely aware of whom your partners need to be and deliberate in your approach to building relationships with them. This is exactly what Nancy did when she reached out to Sharon. She knew Sharon was a key partner and took deliberate steps—visits, involvement in team meetings—to build the partnership.

The partnerships you must build in a matrix role may not be convenient or comfortable. Talking about good relationships in a negotiating setting, Fisher and Brown wrote in *Getting Together: Building Relationships as We Negotiate* (1989): "While it is easier to build a good road across a prairie than through mountains, a good road through mountains may be more valuable than one across a prairie."

Like a road through a mountain, matrix partnerships can be difficult to forge, but the effort pays off if the destination is *mutual benefit*. Without mutual benefit, the attempt to partner can be seen as trying to create pawns or build a network on your way up the corporate ladder. The partnerships we will talk about in this chapter are sustainable, long-term, mutually beneficial partnerships that are built in an earnest way.

In today's multi-tasking, geographically dispersed workforce, most partnerships don't just happen. Even when they do, we tend to be too narrow in our field of partners. Herein lies our starting point:

WHO SHOULD YOUR PARTNERS BE?

"So, Gary, what's the biggest difference between your previous role and this one?" I asked, more as an introductory conversation starter than a formal question to my new client. "There are a hell of a lot more people to piss off in this role." At that point Gary was off and running. He had been in his role one year and had spent the better part of that year stepping on minefields and chasing rabbits down holes.

His relationship requirements had gone from fairly simple, one-dimensional connections with his boss and direct reports to a three-dimensional matrix of potential partners. As with all matrix roles, an endless number of people had to, or wanted to, give input into what he was doing. Gary resented this and reacted by trying to build boundaries. According to Gary, "Why do I need to consult with people in Marketing who know nothing about my area of expertise? They are just slowing me down." Not only did that piss people off (his words, not mine), it was leading him to make decisions and develop work products that missed the mark. In other words, the "mind your own business" approach was failing miserably.

Matrix roles require you to look outside of your team, your silo and your immediate geographic area to identify whom you need to work with and through. It is usually well outside the traditional "us." In Gary's case, he defined "us" as the people who shared his expertise; anyone else was "them" and wasn't allowed in.

> Matrix roles require you to look outside of your team, your silo and your immediate geographic area to identify whom you need to work with and through.
>
> **ZOOM OUT**

But Gary didn't stop there. He also lamented about the junior Marketing folks who were asking him questions and with whom he was supposed to "consult." Frustrated by people below him hounding him, he shut them out. He didn't realize that matrix roles are level neutralizers. You will find yourself interacting and partnering with people at all levels of the organization—up, down, sideways, diagonal. The projects and issues matrix masters find themselves involved in almost always include multiple levels and functions.

So, the lesson of this story—don't be Gary. Strike the right balance between being too limiting in the parameters of whom you work to partner with (and thereby leaving critical people out) and casting too wide of a net (including, to the extreme, making such partnerships superficial and meaningless).

Start by looking at how your role is structured. Every job is divided up differently—yours may be categorized by project, customer or area of responsibility. Then ask yourself about the different people who are involved:

HAND-OFFS	Who do you work hand-in-hand with?
	Who do you hand things off to?
	Who hands things off to you?
WHO HAS...	Power to veto your decisions or implementation of decisions?
	Knowledge, experience or expertise to tap into?
	Opinion leadership that can sway others you need to influence?
	Authority over resources needed to make or implement decisions?
WHO DO YOU NEED TO...	Demonstrate support (in word and deed)?
	Convince or permit others to support?
	Add something to their to-do list?

This list is a snapshot—your list of partners isn't static. It changes by project, as people move in and out of a team or organization, as project scopes shrink or expand and as decisions are made. This exercise is not one that you complete and put on the shelf. Good matrix managers are constantly asking themselves who they should be partnering closely with. You don't need to be attached at the hip with each of these partners—there are gradations of partnerships to consider.

THE MATRIX–PARTNER CONTINUUM™

Partnerships can take many different forms in a matrix ranging from simple hand-offs of information or work products to close integration of tasks and goals. The story of Nancy's two partners illustrates the ends of the continuum: Fran was Nancy's needs-based, low-integration "Dysfunctional Partner," and Sharon was Nancy's relationship-based, high-integration "Integrated Partner."

The vertical axis here is the degree to which partners integrate or organize their work around each other—to what extent they align goals, make decisions and plan based on the other's business. Ryan, a global project leader, defined the highest level of partnering as "when you are willing to change the way you do business or change your goals or your direction based on input and expertise from another person."

The Needs-to-Relationship axis is based on the degree to which the partnership is grounded solely in the business need or extended or enhanced based on the relationship. It is assumed any partnership in a matrix includes a business need (otherwise these relationships are at-will friendships), but movement through this continuum is dependent on extending beyond "I work with you because I need you" to "I work with you because you make me better at what I do."

The type of partnership is based on increasing investments (and return on those investments) in trust, communication and constructive conflict. The first two are obvious—increased trust and communication lead to more relationship-based, integrated partnerships. The third is less obvious because we assume that decreasing conflict is good. As partnerships evolve and integrate, more opportunities for conflict arise. However, if the partnership is strong, the ability to manage and leverage conflict also grows.

THE FOUR MATRIX PARTNERSHIP TYPES

The four types of matrix partnerships—Integrated, Transactional, Collaborative and Dysfunctional—can be seen in any type of matrix role. Here's how I might label the partners of José, a multiple-matrix finance director for an insurance company:

1. INTEGRATED PARTNER
John, VP of Finance (solid line boss):
> *"I am quickly becoming the resident expert on the operations of my business, and he depends on that. I depend on him to look out for my career. I am his go-to person on a lot of things, and I don't hesitate to go to him for counsel on anything. He's gone to bat for me, and I have for him."*

2. COLLABORATIVE PARTNER
Victor, team lead for a cross-functional team José is on:
> *"We have worked together to get this team off the ground—he knows the product, and I bring the financial expertise."*

3. TRANSACTIONAL PARTNER
Barb, General Manager (dotted line boss):
> *"Relationship is fine, I go to her for approvals and reviews as I need to."*

4. DYSFUNCTIONAL PARTNER
Ann, boss of two team members on José's project team:
> *"This one is rough, I feel like I am competing with her for the time and attention of the team members. I say one thing, she says another, and the team is caught in the middle."*

There are two important realities about these partnerships. (1) All types (with the exception of New/Dysfunctional Partnerships) are perfectly acceptable as long as they fit with the business need. (2) When partnerships evolve, they generally do so in baby steps, each level a test to see return on investments in trust, communication and constructive conflict.

INTEGRATED PARTNERS. At the far end of the continuum are Integrated Partners. Your planning, decisions and problem solving involve them. You share advice and counsel. Goals are integrated/calibrated, and communication between partners is integrated into everyday processes. At this level, the partnership may even transcend individuals and be evident at multiple levels in their organizations. You consult and confer on issues that go beyond the obvious connection and business need.

Nancy and Sharon met both key requirements of the Integrated Partner—their planning and execution were harmonized, and they advocated for each other and their teams. They involved and included each other in decision-making on a regular basis. Nancy became an ambassador of sorts for Sharon's team to the manufacturing locations. Sharon added voice to the manufacturing perspective back at headquarters.

COLLABORATIVE PARTNERS. Less discrete tasks and closer coordination are the hallmarks of Collaborative Partners. Hand-offs are supplemented with regular communication to confer and debrief. Not only are there many hand-offs, but some tasks are completed hand-in-hand.

James and Connie are a great example. They brought together two different areas of expertise—IT and nursing, respectively—on a system installation project for a hospital. They were able to bring the needs of both their functions to the table and sort out what was best for the hospital and ultimately the patients. As James put it, "We were able to give and take. I didn't always win and neither did she, but keeping our eye on the prize, we got it done."

> Collaborative Partners focus less on winning individual arguments (and therefore will give in) and more on the big picture wins at the enterprise level.
>
> JUJITSU

Success in these partnerships is reliant on contribution—each partner contributes not only to the work product but to each other's success. Communication surrounds the process—joint planning on the front-end, a continual exchange of information throughout and debriefs at the end of tasks, events or projects. Conflicts are almost always creative in nature (vs. personal), because they are built on the foundation of reliability and trust in the partnership that precedes it. These conflicts are non-threatening and seen as a natural and constructive part of the process.

TRANSACTIONAL PARTNERS. The transactional partner is the classic provider/consumer relationship. The focus is on hand-offs and exchanges. The tasks that connect them are likely process-based, routine and perhaps even repetitive.

Transactional partnerships can be seen in all four types of matrix roles. One of the more natural fits is the reporting relationship matrix role. Dotted line bosses are often transactional partners because of separation by geography or area of expertise. Carrie, a lead for a small business unit within a technology company, is a great example. "Because of the importance of my business to the organization's cash flow, I had a dotted line reporting relationship with the head of Finance. Our connection was strictly on our quarterly numbers; for everything else, I turned to the president of our business." In this example, like all Transactional Partners, the tasks are discrete and involve some exchange of information or work product.

The keys to success in these partnerships are reliability and consistency (which build trust), well-informed partners and addressing conflicts as they arise in a constructive manner. These practices ensure smooth exchanges. A strong transactional partnership is a well-oiled machine.

NEW/DYSFUNCTIONAL PARTNERS. New/Dysfunctional partnerships occur where there is need but no integration. The matrix has brought people or teams together, but they remain separate in terms of their relationship—either because the partnership is too new or because they have fallen into a pattern of competing, comparing or judging the other. Take for example a cross-functional team I worked with several years ago. They were responsible for the design and implementation of a large sales meeting every year. They were trying to figure out how to improve, not their outcome (in their words, "the work product was great") but their process ("it was really painful getting there").

The leads for Sales Training and Meeting Planning were key players in the planning process. When I talked to each of them, they were clearly nowhere near integration. Despite working side-by-side for months leading up to the meeting, they were competing like they were on two different sides on an imaginary battlefield. Second-guessing, blaming and keeping score formed the basis of their relationship. When I asked them individually about "how things went" with the planning of the sales meeting, I could hardly get either of them to talk about anything besides each other.

These two people were critical to the success of the annual meeting, but their dysfunction was making the planning process unbearable to everyone around them. That's the danger of dysfunctional relationships—they are palpable and contagious.

The hallmark of dysfunctional partnerships is lack of trust—which strains communication and turns conflict into competition. The team in this example was lucky that their work product hadn't been affected—yet. They were wise enough to see that despite current success, the level of partnership wasn't sustainable and would eventually start impacting outcomes.

DO YOU HAVE THE RIGHT FIT?

The three functional partnerships can be a pass-through or a destination. A relationship may start off as Transactional but move to Collaborative or Integrated based on business need, time invested and personal connection. Transactional and Collaborative Partnerships are also fine terminal points, because not all partnerships need to evolve to the Integrated level.

The three functional partnership types are also cumulative—not distinct from each other. Any Collaborative Partnership has needs to be met and transactions to conduct. An Integrated Partnership does too, and also requires collaboration. The key is to ensure that the nature of the partnership fits the requirements of the business and that both partners agree as to the desired level of partnership.

"People who feel they are pawns tend to be passive and useless... Slaves are the most inefficient form of labor ever devised by man. If a leader wants to have far-reaching influence, he must make his followers feel powerful and able to accomplish things on their own."

DAVID MCCLELLAND

One team I consulted with was set up as a "committee," that was even in their name, Contract Review Committee. Sitting in on their meetings, it was obvious to me that relationships between the leader and members and among the members were very transactional, partly because they were also a transient team— their membership was constantly changing. They didn't interact much outside their weekly meetings, and their understanding of each other's role and business was very narrow. The goals of the team dictated a closer connection. Because their interaction and knowledge was limited, their meetings were long, with too much explaining, re-explaining and backtracking. Without greater integration, they were struggling in terms of effectiveness and efficiency.

In addition to supporting the business need, partners must be in agreement as to the level of partnership they need. When I explained this to Keith, a U.S. marketing manager working for a Canadian company, he started to laugh. "This explains a lot," he said. "My dotted line boss in Toronto wants to be really involved, asks a lot of questions. It drives me crazy, because I see him as a transactional partner. I go to him on a handful of specific items, and I think he thinks we should be more collaborative, he wants to be involved in much more. We are both assuming the reporting relationship is set up for different reasons."

Let's put one of your partnerships to the "fit test." Think about a partnership you currently have, and specifically about the nature of the work you do in conjunction with the partner. Take this quick assessment:

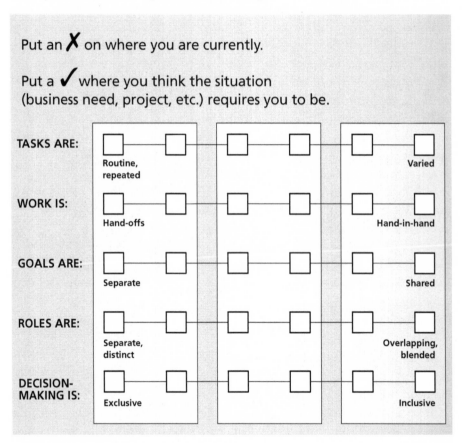

If the majority of the ✓ marks indicating your current needs are in the left column, the situation calls for a Transactional Partnership, the middle a Collaborative Partnership and in the right column an Integrated Partnership.

Now take a look at your ✗s. Are they aligned with the needs? If they are, your partnership is well placed. If they aren't, your partnership needs a fit adjustment—you may be under- or over-investing in a partnership that should ideally be shifted more toward the right (toward Integration) or left (toward Transaction). We will talk about making these shifts in the next section.

THE PARTNERSHIP MINDSET: *DON'T WAIT FOR THEM.*

Steve, a former COO, CFO and now C-level consultant, provides a great illustration of the shifts you need to make to your own point of view before attempting any shifts with a partner:

> *"When I was the division CFO, I got along great with the CEO—Jack, my direct boss. He and I worked wonderfully together. I did not like, nor did I get along with, the corporate CFO, my dotted line guy—his name was Paul. I don't think he liked me, either, and I just tried to avoid him at all costs. At the goal-setting time one year, the CEO said to me, "Steve, in addition to your accountabilities this year, you are going to be evaluated on your ability to create a relationship with Paul." I said, "Jack, that's the worst thing you can ask me to do. I don't like the guy." Jack knew I didn't like the guy, and he said, "Steve, this isn't about trying to create a relationship. This is about absolutely, without question, doing it. You're going to be evaluated on this the rest of the year." So, that was a direct order and I did it. I didn't like it. It was difficult at first. But I kept at it, even when Paul didn't reciprocate. I ended up creating a great relationship with him. The net result of that not only was tremendous success for Paul, for me, for the CEO, but also tremendous sales and earnings breakthroughs. And a lot of it came from that relationship that I created with him. In a matrix role, you have to create relationships even when you don't want to."*

Due in large part to Jack's request, Steve didn't predicate his partnering mindset or behavior on Paul's commitment, values or behavior. In other words, he didn't wait for Paul to change or to initiate improvements. Too often I hear people say that their colleague isn't partnering, so they themselves are unable to partner or feel it would be a waste of time to attempt to partner. This is the biggest mistake you can make. The partnership mindset is: ***Don't wait for them.***

Steve demonstrated the "Don't wait for them" rule beautifully. He initiated the relationship improvement process and didn't predicate his behavior on Paul's.

Sound impossible? Polly Anne-ish? It did to me too at first. A number of books helped me wrap my mind around the idea. It started with an inspirational little book called *The 100/0 Principle* by Al Ritter. The 100 piece of this equation is your behavior; the 0 is what you expect in return. Two books on conflict and negotiations, *The Triangle of Truth* by Lisa Earle McLeod and *Getting Together: Building Relationships as We Negotiate,* by Roger Fisher and Scott Brown of The Harvard Negotiation Project, apply similar models—what Fisher and Brown call being "unconditionally constructive"—to practical applications from parenting to foreign affairs. Anything that applies to nuclear proliferation—which has consequence much more far-reaching than whether or not Sam supports Susie's initiative or Barb and Bob resolve conflicting priorities—surely must have some applications in the work environment.

Still doubting? Let's take a look at your choices if you are in a Dysfunctional Partnership. One of those choices is likely not whether to partner with this person or not. The matrix has brought you together for a business purpose; walking away is probably not in the cards. Your choice lies in where you elect to invest your energy:

To build a strong partnership you invest your energy into constructive actions in line with your values, not fighting fire with fire.

JUJITSU

CHOICE:	ENERGY SPENT ON:
Live with it	Dealing with frustration, extra work required
Fight fire with fire	Strategizing your next move and theirs, executing your combat tactics
Don't wait for them, just change	Constructive actions that are in line with your values

It's a little like buying a home versus renting one—you either give the money away or you invest it. Either way money is spent. In partnerships, *energy* is your currency. You can choose to throw that energy into a black hole (to feed frustration, extra work, strategizing and politicking) or you can invest it in constructive behaviors that are aligned with your values and provide a role model to everyone around you, from your colleagues to your kids. It is your choice.

Before you can make any changes, you have to *change your mindset.* Especially with a Dysfunctional Partnership, you will need to change your mind about your partner. Even in a new partnership, you may need to shed your history from their predecessor or other partnerships you have had.

The first thing you must do is change your mind about your partner.

MINDSET

In the previous story, Steve's boss nudged him into changing his mind about his dysfunctional partner. We don't always have such a force to shift our thinking. Most of the time you will have to dig deep and think differently about the person on your own. If you can't do this, you will not be able to move the partnership. You have to clear your history, which most likely includes all sorts of behaviors, decisions and interactions that have chipped away at trust. You have to replace this history with a simple but powerful thought: "This person is worthy of a partnership." If you have to say it to yourself 500 times a day, it is worth it. Without changing your mind, your actions will be disingenuous and miss the mark. As I stated in the introduction, *trying any of the "how-tos" that form the Essentials before adopting the right mindset will make your efforts disingenuous and limit your outcomes.*

MAKING SHIFTS: FIVE BASELINE INVESTMENTS

Matrix partnerships are funded by gradual increases in trust, communication and constructive conflict. The key here is *gradual* increases. Small investments that help movement from new or Dysfunctional to Transactional partnerships won't help you move to Collaborative or Integrated. Those progressions will require you to compound your investments. A $5 bill into the kids' piggy bank is a substantial investment. A $5 deposit into the college fund is inconsequential. The investments (and the expectation of these investments) expand to scale with the type of partnership. In this section, we will start at the baseline level (equivalent of the piggy bank deposit) and then "compound" with bigger investments in the following section.

When a partnership is new, dysfunctional or starts to slip backwards, some baseline investment is required. I've outlined the five types of baseline investments. You may not need all five in any given situation, nor is there a single magic bullet. Setting or resetting a partnership is not that easy. Here are the Baseline Investments:

1. **Trust them**
2. **Be trustworthy**
3. **Set/reset communication**
4. **Clean up conflicts**
5. **Follow the Help-Me-Help-You Rules**

BASELINE INVESTMENT #1: TRUST THEM. The mindset of "don't wait for them" comes through loud and clear in terms of this first behavior. You can't wait for the other person to trust you. To build trust, you must trust. Trust begets trust. Lack of trust creates more work for yourself (reviewing, controlling, attending to the extreme) and more work for them (covering, justifying, explaining), which only gets you further from trusting.

But think about what trust does—real, resilient trust is hard to defend against. Have you ever *not* trusted someone who unconditionally and genuinely trusted you? Said another way, have you ever trusted someone completely and genuinely when they didn't trust you?

You can't wait for the other person to trust you. To build trust, you must trust.

MINDSET

Even if it's little things, you will have to start trusting them on something. Without this investment, risky as it may be, the partnership will go nowhere.

Here's what demonstrating "I trust you" looks like:

I DON'T TRUST YOU	I TRUST YOU
"I can't be at the meeting, we need to reschedule."	"Go on without me, I don't need to be there."
"I need to see that one more time before I am OK with it."	"I don't need to see it again, go ahead and send it out."
Cc-ing your boss or their boss	Just sending it straight out to them
Holding information until asked	Spontaneously and proactively sharing information
Needing to see it has been done	Assuming it has been done, even when you aren't there to witness it

BASELINE INVESTMENT #2: BE TRUSTWORTHY. Trust is a two-way street. You have to trust them, as well as earn a basic level of trustworthiness, to move out of a Dysfunctional Partnership or initiate a new partnership. When I asked Steve about where he started with Paul, he said he just started with the bare bone basics, "I made sure I was reliable and consistent, and when I wasn't, I acknowledged it."

Reliability and consistency in a partnership means simple things like responding to questions, being on time, delivering the work product you said you would, making decisions that are in line with what you have said and done previously. And when you fail to be reliable and consistent, acknowledge it. The only thing worse than doing something that calls into question your reliability or consistency is failing to acknowledge it. People will think that you either didn't see the incongruity or assumed they wouldn't notice. If you waver on your commitments, be transparent about it or you risk digging yourself deeper into a difficult trust rebuilding situation.

If you waver on your commitments, be transparent about it or you risk digging yourself deeper into a difficult trust rebuilding situation.

JUJITSU

BASELINE INVESTMENT #3: SET / RESET COMMUNICATION. Essential #6 covers what assumptions to avoid in this process, but for now let's just talk about initial and recovery steps as applied to communication. Start with the basics. All you need to focus on here (like reliability and consistency in resetting trust) is informing—make sure they get the information they need.

To set/reset communication:

1. **Acknowledge:** Recognize your communication may have been lacking in the past and what issues that may have caused (in the case of an existing relationship).

2. **Ask:** Ask your partners what they need to know and how they want to find out. Then continue asking whether your communication is working for them.

3. **Plan:** Agree on a communication plan that outlines what, when and how.

4. **Get into a rhythm:** Cadence in communication is important. A consistent rhythm of communication (like weekly emails with a consistent, easy-to-read format or monthly discussions with a set agenda) drives comfort and trust.

5. **Careful of the "out of sight out of mind" trap:** Your matrix is likely to be physically scattered. Don't rely on the "who you see" method of remembering what and who you need to communicate with. Those who you don't run into are more easily overlooked.

JoAnne, a sales support manager, told me about some seemingly innocuous check-in meetings that got things back on track with the sales managers she worked with in the field:

> *"I sensed things were slipping, and so I instituted monthly check-ins with them. They insisted they were too busy, but I made sure I kept pushing and asked a lot of questions about what would be helpful for both of us. We went over progress, where we were on different initiatives and what was on the horizon. We brainstormed solutions to issues we had—I almost always walked out with a better way to work with them. It kept us informed, focused and on track*

in terms of our shared goals and who was doing what. We were all much more ready to be proactive because we were on top of things. After about four cycles, I felt things start to shift. We regained our confidence in each other and even comfort—it just made it easier to get things done."

JoAnne hit on many of the five set/reset behaviors. She also persisted and focused on making the check-ins meaningful not just for her but for her partners as well.

What she didn't do was wait for them to admit that they had been lousy communicators too or to ask her what communication she needed. She just focused on informing and kept doing it. She didn't waste energy identifying their shortfalls, only channeled energy into doing the right thing on her end.

BASELINE INVESTMENT #4: CLEAN UP CONFLICT. If you are in a Dysfunctional Partnership, most likely you have been stockpiling. When you stockpile, you don't address a conflict, you store it. Sometimes you sweep conflicts under a rug; other times you stockpile and then dump them on your partner when you have reached a breaking point. Or maybe you are stockpiling and spreading—telling everyone but the person you have the conflict with.

Nancy was definitely stockpiling with Fran. Years later, when retelling the Tale of Two Partners to me, she vividly remembered the conflicts, the confrontations and even specific contentious conversations. At the time she thought it was the right thing to do—at first because she didn't want to rock the boat, later because she had given up hope of fixing things.

Stockpiling is a partnership killer. Even if you are not dumping or spreading the word, you can't hide stockpiling. You may think that what you are holding on to doesn't come out in how/what you communicate, how you make decisions or how you behave in general, but it does.

To reset a Dysfunctional Partnership, you have to clear the slate—either by truly letting go and forgiving or by clearing the air.

What do you let go and forgive? The things that have low impact—*today*. It may have been a big deal six months ago, but if it is not consequential now, let it go. Also let go of things that happened once, but aren't indicative of the partnership. You don't have to overtly forgive your partner, but mentally delete it. No longer spend any time thinking about it or talking about it. Truly let go.

Decide what to let go or tackle based on present impact and frequency of the behavior.

TRIAGE

Tackle those things that have high impact today—whether they happened once or a hundred times. If it impacts current results or trust in the relationship, you need to bring it up in a way that builds the partnership.

Two books that I recommend often when it comes to tricky matrix conversations are *Crucial Conversations* and *Crucial Confrontations* by Patterson, et al. (2002, 2005). These two books offer some of the most practical, realistic advice on difficult dialogue. The approach they prescribe is especially relevant to matrix relationships because of the focus, not just on resolving the conflict, but actually strengthening the relationship as a result.

> *"Trust is like the air we breathe. When it's present, nobody really notices. But when it's absent, everybody notices."*
>
> WARREN BUFFET

New partnerships don't come with a bag full of issues to resolve, but discussing potential conflicts and how to deal with them up front might make sense. It is amazing how a brief comment like, "Along the way we will probably disagree on how to manage corporate resources" makes addressing the conflict easy, safe and objective when it actually occurs. The conflict shifts from being a big deal, something that you didn't see coming or that was initiated by one partner, to something you knew would come up and you are ready to move through swiftly.

BASELINE INVESTMENT #5: HELP-ME-HELP-YOU RULES. There is a classic line from the movie *Jerry Maguire* that describes another set of baseline investments. Jerry Maguire implores his new client to "help me help you." Good matrix partners are good customers and providers who tend to abide by a few general rules that promote good working relationships. Mark, an account rep in a Customer Hub Matrix, shared this story:

> *"I had a proposal that needed to get out to a client and went to the gal that drafts these for me. When I walked up, I could tell she was rushed. After talking to her I found out that she was indeed under the gun. She told me that she had three proposals to get out that day. I knew mine could wait 24 hours so I didn't cry wolf and tell her mine was just as urgent. I said, "Well, you know what, mine can wait until tomorrow, why don't you take care of those three and then let's talk tomorrow." It was the right thing to do, but it also told her that I don't call everything urgent—and when I do, it's for real."*

Mark's example is a great one for several of the Help-Me-Help-You Rules. Here are the rules and what they look like from a provider and customer perspective:

THE HELP-ME-HELP-YOU RULES	PROVIDER PERSPECTIVE	CUSTOMER PERSPECTIVE
Don't cry wolf, ever	Don't overstate the degree of difficulty of filling a request	Don't overstate the urgency or importance of your request
Know their business	Know their business and anticipate their needs	Know and respect their processes and deadlines and make sure your request reflects this understanding. Do not expect them to make exceptions to their rules and processes, especially if your poor planning created the situation.
Co-own any failures	Rarely are there just lessons to be learned on one side only, chances are both the provider and customer have adjustments to make	
Don't assume priorities are known or shared	Don't assume that just because you work in the same organization, your partner already understands your priorities. They may have no knowledge or appreciation of the work that you do outside your relationship with them.	Don't assume that just because you work in the same organization, your partner understands your priorities already. Realize you aren't their only priority: know how your request fits into overall workflow and workload.

COMPOUNDING YOUR INVESTMENT

We're now entering the land of more substantial and riskier investments, with bigger potential returns. No more piggy banks and $5 bills or moving from New/Dysfunctional to Transactional Partnerships. These are shifts that move a Transactional to Collaborative Partnership or Collaborative to Integrated. Your portfolio at this level involves: Advocating, Including and Leveraging.

COMPOUNDING YOUR INVESTMENT: ADVOCATE. Remember the role that Nancy and Sharon played for each other? Nancy was Sharon's advocate to the manufacturing team, and Sharon provided an additional voice from Nancy's team to corporate. Being an advocate means you are their eyes and ears, ambassador and supporter, and they are yours—you go above and beyond mere helping and appreciating or being a good team player:

GOOD TEAM PLAYERS...	INTEGRATED PARTNERS...
Help out when asked	See when their help is needed and jump in
Solve a problem that is brought to them	See problems and bring them to light for their partner
Thank partners for a great job	Let others know what an outstanding partner they are
Let partners know when things aren't going quite right	Help partners figure out how to fix a problem

The right hand column outlines some behaviors that have the potential to compound investments in terms of the trust between two partners. Advocating is much more proactive than other partnership behaviors and much more hands-on, which is what makes it more risky but infinitely more potent. It is nearly impossible not to want to partner with someone who is your advocate.

COMPOUNDING YOUR INVESTMENT: INCLUDE. I conducted a number of focus groups for a hospital client looking to understand how they could increase the partnership level with their physicians. They had made a concerted effort over the previous 12 months to communicate better with physicians, but still felt that they were disconnected. After talking to 50+ doctors, the answer was simple—in fact, so simple that the administration questioned my results. The doctors wanted to be included. They wanted to be included in decisions, brought into problem solving. The administration had increased the information going out, so the physicians were informed—but that only got them so far (to the Transactional Partnership level). For the doctors, information wasn't enough. The hospital needed to compound it's investment—they needed to include.

Including people in meetings, involving them in decisions and problem solving and sharing information tells them you not only trust them, you value them. And the bonus is that this inclusion will also improve the quality of those meetings and decisions.

COMPOUNDING YOUR INVESTMENT: LEVERAGE CONFLICT. Progressing through the levels of partnership is more than just dealing with tactical or interpersonal conflicts as they come up, it requires *leveraging* conflict.

Leveraging starts with realizing that the existence of conflicts is not an indictment of the partnership, the structure or the person. Conflicts demonstrate the reason the matrix was formed in the first place. In that tension between corporate and local, marketing and sales, field and home office, lies the right answer for the business. Leveraging, not ignoring or minimizing the conflict, puts that tension to use.

What does leveraging conflict look like? Essentials #2 and #3 cover resolving conflict in terms of goals and roles—which are the most common conflicts in matrix roles. Essential #4 covers conflicts in decision-making. The common threads that underlie conflict in all of these con-

To successfully solve a problem, view it at the enterprise level, not your personal silo level.

ZOOM OUT

texts is getting it on the table, viewing from a problem (not personal) and enterprise (not individual silo) perspective and staying in the conversation (versus cutting it short or avoiding it).

A project team I observed had this down to an art form. Their sole purpose, every meeting and every item on their agenda, was about resolving conflicts. Representing six different sub-projects, they were tasked with approving additional project resources and shifting project resources as needed. The first thing I noticed was that it was nearly impossible to identify what function the team members represented. There was no overt lobbying for their project's specific needs or preferences. In fact, they would often pull in information or ask questions from the other's viewpoints. They continually reminded each other what "the prize" was—what the enterprise-level project needed from them. This doesn't mean they didn't conflict—in fact, that is all they did. But they didn't short-change it; they leveraged the conflicts and appreciated that that was their job—to bring it all together and hash it out.

Matrix roles are made up of intersections—organizational paths that can't run in parallel but must cross. Conflict at these intersections is inevitable. The key is not to avoid the conflicts, but leverage them to get to better outcomes.

PULLING BACK: WHEN YOUR PARTNERSHIP OVERREACHES

Usually the business requires a more advanced partnership than the two partners are exhibiting, but there can be times where your level of partnership actually exceeds requirements. This may not seem like a bad thing, but here's what you should look out for:

- How do others see it? Do they view the partnership as favoritism? Does it make them question your motives?
- Are you using your energy wisely? Is the energy better spent on partnerships that more closely align with business needs?

- Does overshooting the partnership lead you down the wrong path? Is this partner more influential than he or she should be in terms of how you get results?

We all have our version of A Tale of Two Partners. At any given time we will have partnerships that cover the continuum from new or Dysfunctional to Integrated. Fit matters. So does your mindset. And whether measured by small deposits or significant investments, change in a partnership starts with you. The partnerships you build will support, if not guarantee, goal alignment, which is the first major "to do" in matrix mastery and our Essential #2.

IN SUMMARY

EMBRACE

→ Partnerships are the way work gets done in matrix roles.

→ Many people are involved in your work: let them in. Don't spend energy blocking them out.

→ Partnerships require increasing investments in trust, communication and constructive conflict.

→ Don't wait for your partner to change or initiate the change—it's up to you.

TRY

→ Take a critical look at who you should be partnering with. Start by looking at how your role is structured and identify who is key in each of your areas of responsibility.

→ Assess the level of your key partnerships. What does the business call for? Is the partnership up to the task?

→ Initiate a baseline investment or compound your investment in one or two of your key partnerships over the next three weeks. See how the dynamics shift.

IN PRACTICE

REPORTING RELATIONSHIP MATRIX

In a reporting relationship role, your relationship with the two bosses looks different—it must. You will find yourself doing much more partnering with them than in a traditional role, especially when one has a different area of expertise than you (as is often the case). You may even find yourself in the middle of their partnership. Although you can't make them like each other, you can't add to their issues, and you may even need to take steps to help repair their partnership. For this you will need to Flex Your Influence Muscle (Essential #5).

CUSTOMER HUB MATRIX

You most likely have many Transactional Partners, each providing you with products and information you need for your customer (be they internal or external). Be careful not to discount how engaged and motivated they need to be to help you. In other words, the business need may appear to be Transactional, but to get full engagement and focus from these partners, invest in some inclusion and advocacy (especially the recognition portion of advocacy).

CROSS-FUNCTIONAL AND PROJECT TEAM MATRICES

You will clearly have some level of partnership with those on your teams. If you are the team leader, don't forget their bosses! They are important partners too. Be careful not to be satisfied with Transactional Partners on a team—rarely can teams remain at this level. Whether you are the lead or a team member, take steps toward collaboration by sharing information readily and including team members in meetings and decisions.

"Every day you spend drifting away from your goals is a waste not only of that day, but also the additional day it takes to regain lost ground."

RALPH MARSTON

ESSENTIAL #2
GET GOALS ALIGNED

You have to start with **PARTNERSHIPS** to get...

GOALS ALIGNED	**FLEX YOUR INFLUENCE MUSCLE**
ROLES CLEAR	**COMMUNICATE WITHOUT ASSUMPTION**
DECISIONS MADE	**TREAT MEETINGS LIKE THEY MATTER**

All of this requires you to...

MINDSET   JUJITSU   ZOOM OUT   TRIAGE

WHAT IT IS

When working at organizational intersections, misalignments are unavoidable—sometimes even intentional. To master the matrix you must be artful in bringing together those misalignments with the potential to be constructive, while also vigilant in identifying and resolving conflicts with the potential to derail.

WHAT YOU WILL LEARN

» Two types of matrix goal misalignments
» Four ground rules for goal alignment
» Setting and aligning goals from the start, and realigning as you go
» Channeling and cultivating natural misalignments
» Preventing and resolving man-made misalignments

JIM is a marketing director, and one of his roles involves leading a cross-functional team that drives a complex, ongoing approval process involving Sales, Marketing, R&D, Legal and several scientific functions. This eight-person team—representing each of the eight functions in the process—is charged with approving promotional material that must be scientifically exact, legally sound, in accordance with all regulatory requirements, aligned with the marketing strategy and, ultimately, effectively sell the product. Each representative on the team has a different idea of what makes "good" promotional material and a different goal regarding what the material needs to be. The perfect promotional material from a legal perspective makes no sense to a marketer. Left to their devices, sales would throw in anything that might lead to a sale, and the scientists would come up with promotional content that made sense only to them. Eight different goals, eight different agendas—an eight-way intersection with Jim in the middle serving as traffic cop meant endless meetings and an approval time that was measured in months.

Janet is a director of Finance, with a solid line reporting relationship to Marcia, the VP of Finance for her division, and a dotted line reporting relationship to Kenneth, the VP of Manufacturing for the division. It is May; five months into the fiscal year, and things are humming along as planned for Janet and her team. Then Kenneth stops by and informs Janet that one of his top goals for the year requires some fairly detailed, customized financial reports. He will need Janet and her team to design them and provide them on a monthly basis, perhaps weekly basis, beginning next month. As Kenneth is talking, Janet is acutely aware of the Finance function's Top Five Goals, which are posted on the bulletin board in her office. On the top of that list is the goal to standardize all financial reports globally. A goal of standardization and a goal requiring customization: which one will win out?

If you have been in a matrix role for a period of time, you have faced competing goals like Jim and Janet. In fact competing goals was the #1 challenge identified by the 100+ matrix managers who took part in the research for this book.

Competing goals was the #1 challenge reported by matrix practitioners.

SURVEY

THE TWO TYPES OF MATRIX GOAL MISALIGNMENTS

As we've already talked about, organizations want the best of both worlds, so they set up teams and reporting relationships that bring different sides together to produce solutions that benefit the enterprise as a whole. In part, misalignments are common because matrix roles exist to create goal collisions. This is the type of misalignment that Jim's team faced every day. The organization didn't want a solution based on the goals of only one function, but for the organization as a whole. It wanted a solution that achieved the goals of Sales *and* Marketing *and* Legal, etc.—thus the cross-functional team.

Natural misalignments are not the only goal clashes prevalent in matrix roles. Because these roles exist in complex organizations and operate within multiple matrices, misalignments also occur because we forget to communicate, assume alignment or let goals drift until they collide. I call these *man-made* misalignments, the "man" here coming from the Latin "manus," or "hand," not male—we females are equally guilty of creating misalignments! This is the dilemma Janet was faced with. She was in a matrix role because the organization didn't want a finance team that focused exclusively on technical expertise or one engulfed by the business it supported. It wanted a team that was technically adept *and* steeped in the realities of the business—thus the dual-reporting relationship. But in this case, the connection between the two parts of the matrix was frayed, goals drifted, and a misalignment was created.

> *"One half of knowing what you want is knowing what you must give up before you get it."*
>
> SIDNEY HOWARD

Behind each dispute lies significant time and effort—spent by already stretched resources—to realign and reprioritize. Whether natural or man-made, unless you work through misalignments, you and your partners will be paddling in two different directions: you'll end up exhausted, but in the same place. And "in the same place" is definitely not where anyone wants to land at milestone time.

FOUR GROUND RULES FOR GOAL ALIGNMENT

Four basic ground rules in goal alignment can help you whether you are tackling a goal conflict that is inherent to your matrix role or one that sprouted up while no one was looking.

IT'S BIGGER THAN YOU. I use a great exercise with matrix teams that pits the goals of two people against the goals of everyone else in the room. The details aren't important, but suffice it to say that throughout the game, participants must choose between options that earn the most points for their pair and options that earn the most points for the whole group (usually four pairs) but mean less for their individual pair. What participants don't realize until the end is that every individual pair will maximize their own points if they all consistently choose the option that earns the most points for the whole group. Having run this exercise dozens of times, it is clear that our natural inclination is to do what is right for our pair. Whether based on proximity (each pair sits together, about 6–8 feet from the others) or the fact that it is easier to align with one other person than seven, our natural inclination is to think small and immediate. We tend to define "team" rather narrowly.

In a matrix role there is always an overarching goal—bigger than you, sometimes even bigger than your team, function or geography—that takes precedence over any individual goals. If you go in determined to maximize your personal success or your immediate team's success, the matrix breaks down. There is an "and," not an "or," at the heart of

You have to look broadly to see the "and" at the heart of every matrix goal.

ZOOM OUT

every matrix goal—forgetting or ignoring this will lead to sub-optimal results as well as sub-optimal relationships.

BE REALISTIC. Optimists beware—realism is required when aligning matrix goals. You can't run after all competing goals, even though you will be tempted to try, according to a study done by researchers Cantor and Blanton in 1999. They found that highly optimistic people push forward and try to accomplish competing goals because they don't want to follow the more obvious path to resolving goal conflict—which is to give up or at least reduce commitment to one of the conflicting goals. Optimism is an admirable trait that can get you through many challenging situations. But with the multitude of competing goals in a matrix role, you cannot afford to be so optimistic that you don't make tough choices (or ask that those choices be made for you).

Be realistic about the degree to which you can/should chase after competing goals.

MINDSET

BE READY TO MAKE TRADE-OFFS.
Without willingness to make trade-offs, an intersection team like Jim's is doomed to fail. They need to keep in mind that the situation is "bigger than them," and maintaining a good dose of realism is necessary for the next step—trade-offs.

Making a trade-off has the potential to loosen others up—psychologically, most people will feel the need to repay in kind.

JUJITSU

There will absolutely be compromises, some (perhaps many) that you will have to make yourself. Going in to a conflict assuming that trade-offs will take place automatically shifts what you say and how you say it, and this change can't help but shift outcomes. Not only will your willingness to make trade-offs shift the outcome of the discussion at hand, but future disputes as well. Making a trade-off has the potential to loosen others up—psychologically, most people will feel the need to repay in kind.

ASSUME NOTHING. Operating at high-speed, Janet didn't slow down to make sure she and Kenneth were in sync on annual goals. And Kenneth assumed that any goal of his was Janet's as well. These assumptions helped them pick up speed, but tripped them up in the end. The ambiguity that surrounds matrix roles and the speed at which we work leads us to rely on assumptions—they function as shortcuts. However, these assumptions are the main ingredient for goal misalignments, when, for example, we assume that others know our goals, assume that our priority is their priority or assume that goals aligned at the beginning of the year are still aligned seven months later. Assume nothing. If your matrix is above you, don't assume your bosses are aligned. If you are working in a matrix around you, don't assume your goal or priority is shared by others. Ask questions, share information and clarify. Essential #6 covers assumptions in communication in full, in all matrix contexts, but it holds a special place in goal alignment.

ALIGN FROM THE START AND THEN REALIGN AS YOU GO

Jim and Janet share a common need to align with their matrix partners right from the start. For Jim, whose team is set up to collide, his goal is to cultivate these perspectives into work products that maximize the organization effectively and efficiently. Aligning from the start will help this team find common ground, so they can better cultivate the conflicts that really matter.

For Janet, her misalignment happened because wires were crossed, or maybe things shifted and the owners of the goals didn't think to realign with stakeholders. Someone took their eye off the ball, got caught up in their part of the world and didn't look up to see who needed to be aligned around their goal. For Janet, aligning from the start will help *prevent* misalignments.

Alignment begins with setting goals and relies on sticking to a finite number of goals that are kept in the forefront. As one leader who took part in the research for this book put simply, "You must have a huge focus on a few things." There are three requirements that set the foundation for goal alignment in matrix roles: include the right people, land on a limited set of goals and keep goals in the foreground. You must have all three to ensure alignment. Here's what happens when you don't:

INCLUDE THE RIGHT PEOPLE	LAND ON A LIMITED SET OF GOALS	KEEP GOALS IN THE FOREGROUND	RESULTS:
✓	✓	✓	*GOAL ALIGNMENT*
✓	✓		Distractions, drifting
✓		✓	Diffused efforts
	✓	✓	Stakeholder resistance

INCLUDE THE RIGHT PEOPLE. Remember Mary and Fran in The Tale of Two Partnerships? They had given up including and started just throwing goals and decisions over the fence at each other. With every missed opportunity for inclusion, resentment built up and trust faded. What they were missing was the fact that when you set up goals with the help of those people who will actually support them or have a stake in them, the goals are always going to be more realistic and better understood. You will also be developing goals that people actually feel some ownership over. These goals stand a decent chance of survival in ever-changing multi-dimensional organizations. Goals set behind closed doors, with just those in your sandbox or silo, risk diminished relevance and practicality, not to mention resentment when people believe they were excluded, forgotten or discounted.

The ideal situation for setting goals involves having all interested parties in the room, but that's rarely possible due to timing, geography and other practicalities. Start by identifying the key people to involve. There are probably more than you think. For example, if you are setting goals for a team, including your team members is obvious. But what about their solid line bosses? Don't miss an opportunity to build their understanding and showcase their support for the project. In any event, identify the key people and push to have a few others. Those who you can't get in the room can be involved in another way—ask them to be a sounding board or a reviewer.

There are probably more people to include in goal setting than you think.

ZOOM OUT

Let participants know how they will be used—are they giving you input so you can set the goals? Or are you bringing the group in to reach consensus on the goals? There is a big difference between these two purposes, and you need to let them know which type it is upfront.

Your goal-setting process needs to be inclusive, as does your goal communication process. There will be people who need to know your goals because they impact their own goals. If you have levels beneath you, your goals will need to be cascaded so that others can identify the priorities and feed their goals into yours. If you have a matrix around you, think of any others who should know about your goals—especially people who you may need to pull in or hand off to.

LAND ON A LIMITED SET OF GOALS. Select, restricted, limited. These are all good words to describe the goals you set for yourself or your matrix team. I don't recommend a specific number of goals, because whenever I was asked in the past, organizations ran with whatever magic number I mentioned. The problem was that they didn't truly go out and create, say, five great goals. They simply tried to roll 50 goals into five. What I can tell you is, the ideal number is a heck of a lot smaller than you think.

Maintaining alignment across your matrix is impossible with a laundry list of goals. If you want tight alignment and maximum focus, decrease the number of goals you have to pursue. The number of goals you create at the beginning of the year correlates to the conversation you have at the end of the year. The fewer goals, the more likely your conversation revolves around how much you accomplished. The more goals, the more likely your conversation focuses on how much you didn't finish and how many you just plain forgot about. I have yet to work with a client who at the end of the year said they didn't set enough goals at the beginning of the year.

> *"The pessimist complains about the wind; the optimist expects it to change; the realist adjusts the sails."*
>
> WILLIAM ARTHUR WARD

How do you get to a handful? Stack them. Create criteria based on the highest-level goals and strategies of the organization and rank them. Be brutal, and apply that brutality to determine your threshold. Above the line is in the mix, below the line falls out (but save the list for next year—this is your starting point). Then hang on to those rankings—you will use them all year to make tough calls about what you or your team does. Alternatively, you can use an ABC prioritization (A=must have; B=need to have; C=nice to have), *if* you have parameters on how many (or what percent) you will have in each category. Without these limits, everything becomes an A priority. Whatever you do, compare goals to each other, not just to your criteria, and force yourself to make difficult choices.

Finally, test your list with a few independent, objective outsiders—people completely outside of the process who will not be involved in executing the goals. Walk them through your criteria, your list and the rationale for your rankings or ratings. These bystanders can match goals directly to criteria, not through the filter of history, politics or emotions.

KEEP GOALS IN THE FOREGROUND. "Out of sight out of mind" is the reality for many goals set with high expectations in a conference room at the beginning of the year. It is even more so for the goals that criss-cross yours. Chances are Kenneth—Janet's partner who was unknowingly declaring war on Janet's functional goals—heard something about some Finance goal in January, but didn't hear about it again and forgot when he went gung-ho into his own initiative. Once you have set the goals, the real work begins—not just in working toward the goals, but in keeping focused. If you have picked a limited number of meaningful goals, this shouldn't be hard. If you have picked too many or they lack relevance, your focus is sure to wander before the ink is dry on your goal document.

Keeping goals in the foreground helps prevent the drift and shift that leads to slipping back into silo thinking, "what's right for me." For one team I worked with, the collective goal boiled down to: *vanilla*. They were installing a new system and every time someone started down the path of "my function needs the system to be customized to do blah, blah, blah" the group reminded them that their target was *vanilla*—a plain, non-customized system that could be easily supported by the vendor. They kept that collective goal in the forefront by constantly reminding themselves of it.

Here are three very simple ways to keep goals in the foreground:

1. Make goals visible to everyone. In the example above, *vanilla* was a verbal reminder, but physical reminders can be equally powerful. Bulletin boards, white boards, screen savers, shared drives, collaboration sites, posters, laminated cards, tattoos, whatever it takes. And in whatever form—scorecards, list, spreadsheets. Don't bury your goals in a binder or some subfolder on your computer. Keep your goals and your progress visible—doing this shows that you are serious about the goal, it isn't going away and "Hey look, we are actually getting traction on this."

2. Use goals to filter priorities. Goals should be used to drive actions and decisions on what work should be done and when. I can't say this any clearer than Gene, a project lead on a large global initiative:

> *"In the team meetings I remind everyone, 'What you're*
> *working on should be driving to one of these goals, and*
> *if it's not you should be having a conversation with me*
> *or your manager about it. We need to make sure that at*
> *the end of the year we can look back and say number*
> *one, we did everything we needed to do to achieve the*
> *goals that have been set out either for you individually or*
> *for us as a team. Two, anything that we did that didn't*
> *support those goals was a justified, conscious decision.'"*

Pamela, a project manager in a large multinational pharmaceuticals company, tells a similar story on a larger scale:

> *"It sounds really simplistic, but we have a ranked list from*
> *number one to however many projects are going on at that*
> *time. Everyone has access to this information, and it is*
> *updated at least quarterly. So if you are working on #4 and*
> *someone comes in and asks you to drop everything for num-*
> *ber #14, your response is pretty obvious. That doesn't mean*
> *you don't talk about it, but nine times out of 10 you end up*
> *sticking with #4 and the conversation is pretty short."*

3. Use goals as a framework. Your goals are not just a reference, but also an organizing framework for the year. All meetings, whether they are informal one-on-ones, monthly team meetings or large quarterly powwows, should have an agenda structured around the goals and outcomes focused on the goals. Everything you do and communicate should be structured around the same few goals.

New goals and realities will always come up, and when goals must shift make sure you shift them purposefully. Don't just let them drift and assume everyone is following the drift. Be as conscious about resetting goals as you were about setting them in the first place. Communicate the shift broadly so that people can adjust their individual goals and priorities. Also prepare yourself for people's responses. Some will take the change in stride; others will question it. One of the leaders I talked to described goal realignment as feeling "like your base just became unsteady; like your foundation just moved under your feet." Be ready to support your team through the shift.

The guidelines here are your starting point, but no amount of pre-alignment is going to eliminate collisions. To be effective in truly managing matrix goals, you have to be very adept at **channeling and cultivating** the inherent conflicts into solutions that maximize the big picture goal, **preventing** those conflicts that are caused by neglect and, for those that slip past you, **resolving** through your own devices or other's.

CHANNELING AND CULTIVATING NATURAL MISALIGNMENTS

Let's go back to Jim, the traffic cop in a cross-functional team's eight-way intersection. There were actually multiple "Jims" in this organization, a total of five teams with this same configuration and end goal. I observed all of them in an effort to help them "manage conflict better." If you have been paying attention so far, you know that these teams were the nucleus of naturally occurring and purposeful goal collision. They didn't need to "manage" conflict—they needed to channel it in a way that helped them reach their collective goal more effectively and efficiently.

Some teams were better than others, and one team really stood out. Here's what that team did differently:

- They didn't personalize the conflict. They didn't attack the opinions of others or feel the need to defend their own. They channeled their disagreements toward their desired end.

- They constantly went back to the big picture. Not just the team leader, but team members always reframed things, "Well if our goal is to…"

- They took each other's perspective. The marketing person asked legal questions, the regulatory rep brought up clinical issues. It was hard for me to tell who came from which function—they were all concerned with coming up with solutions that made sense from all angles.

- They used their trump cards (flat out disagreement) wisely and sparingly. Because they conserved these, it packed a powerful punch when they put their foot down.

- When a team member refuted something, they had a follow-up suggestion. They focused on what could be done and what possible options were available.

- They got everything on the table. If a perspective wasn't coming out, they asked the person or someone else offered it up.

The team leader made sure there was time set aside to hear everyone's perspectives and modeled the desired behaviors. It was clear that everyone shared his mindset. When I asked the team leader what he did, he said some of their "ground rules" were set up formally, but most were just based on having the right people on the team to model behaviors and the others following suit. In his words, "Those who have a different definition of 'team' pretty much stick out like a sore thumb."

To use the language from Essential #1—this team was clearly a group of Integrated Partners. They had learned not only to deal with conflict, but to actually use it to their advantage in delivering their work product.

PREVENTING MAN-MADE GOAL MISALIGNMENTS

Now we return to Janet, stuck between two goals: standardization of process and customization of reports. Both she and Kenneth, her dotted line supervisor, were carrying around assumptions about their goals and either didn't align at the beginning or didn't check in with each other later to make sure they were still aligned.

Here's what she could have done to *prevent* the goal conflict:

Make the hunt for misalignments everyone's job: Individuals in matrix positions are the recipients of goals/priorities from other parts of the organization, and as such, have a unique point of view. Often they are the only ones who see misalignments that are occurring or about to occur. As one leader put it, if you are in a matrix role, you have to "be on the hunt" for priorities that conflict, goals that collide and timelines that clash. Furthermore, you have to be willing to bring these up. As a team leader, you have to make it clear that transparency is key and that calling attention to competing goals is not only OK but necessary for problem solving.

Create a forum: Even in a matrix role, you can't see all sides; alignments can only be found through dialogue with your bosses, team and peers. Create a forum for this and do it on a regular basis. Maybe it will take place at the end of each weekly meeting or at the end of a one-to-one— whatever it looks like, make it a practice to bring up misalignments and ask others about what they are seeing. Ask questions: Is there any new information that would lead to a misalignment? New projects or initiatives that have been added? Timelines that are changing? This constant scanning catches misalignments before they crash and turn ugly. Dealing with conflicts as they approach is easier and less emotional than waiting until they're right in front of you.

Look for early warning signs: What are some signs that goals are starting to drift for someone in your matrix? Maybe they miss meetings or start delegating the meetings to someone else, or their response time extends. These signs should tell you that something else is drawing their attention away. When attention strays, goals drift. When you see an early warning sign, bring it up directly to the person. Start with, "I noticed..." Get an understanding of what is pulling them. Reiterate the importance of the goal and address how you can get things back on track.

RESOLVING MAN-MADE MISALIGNMENTS: PICK YOUR BATTLES

When a misalignment manages to evade early detection, like Janet and Kenneth's, you have some choices for how to resolve it. In the introduction we introduced a building block called "Triage." Here's what triage looks like in goal alignment:

Pick your battles based on timeframe and impact.

TRIAGE

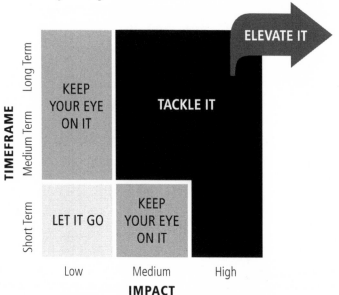

You have to consider impact and timeframe. If a goal conflict doesn't have a big impact on you or the team, just let it go and carry the conflict—work both goals. The bigger the impact and the longer it will stay in conflict, the more likely you are to need to directly resolve it. For the really big issues, you may attempt to resolve, but if that fails your back-up strategy may be to elevate to a person with more influence or authority.

PARTNERSHIP-DRIVEN RESOLUTION

In the case of Janet and Kenneth, which is a true story from an interview, here's how the conflict played out:

> Once I realized Kenneth's expectations and the collision course they were on with Finance's goals, I considered my options. Kenneth is a pretty persuasive guy, and the easy thing would have been to just have my team jump in and start designing and producing the reports for him. We would have looked like heroes to Manufacturing, but would have been scolded by the Finance function. Or I could have taken it to my boss and had him deal with it, which would have really made Kenneth mad. Or I could have launched into my well-rehearsed spiel about the importance of the Finance function's vision of "one financial report globally," which Kenneth cares nothing about and which would have built up resentment between the two functions.
>
> I ended up just asking a bunch of questions. I wanted to get a clear understanding of what he needed. I knew his business well, so I could push a little and say things like, "Are you sure that is what you need, because here's what I have seen you use." I came out of this with a really good sense of his needs—I think he even understood his needs better. Then I laid the Finance goal on the table. And I basically turned to him and said, "This is where I am being pulled. I can easily get you this and this, but this is outside the parameters of what the Finance function is asking me to do. Can you live with this so that I can do what is right for both functions?" We have a good relationship, and he's been in a matrix role before,

so that helped, but in the end I was able to give him the
85% of what he wanted that lined up with Finance's
goals, and he learned to live without the other 15%.

Janet and Kenneth recovered nicely—their steps toward resolution were much better than their preventative measures. Here's what Janet and Kenneth did right:

Don't just "take the mountain": Janet didn't just take Kenneth's request at face value and run with it. Had she tried to hold both goals, she would have ended up failing on at least one of them, and the trust and credibility of her team would have been shot.

Ask questions to clarify: Because Janet paused and didn't just take the mountain, she was able to ask questions to make sure she understood Kenneth's goal, if/how it collided with hers, and eventually that information led to a solution that made sense for both of them. What is important to remember here is that *when you think you have the full picture, ask more questions.* What sounds like a misalignment may not be when you really dig into the request. Sometimes clarification, not resolution, is what a situation calls for. At the very least you will have a much clearer sense of what and where the disconnect is, which will help you choose a tactic for resolution.

Consider your options: Again, because Janet paused and used that opportunity to learn more about the misalignment, she was able to think through her options. She didn't just take the mountain, but she didn't automatically elevate it to her boss either. Both of those are easy, short-term fixes. She chose the tougher but ultimately more rewarding path— attempting to resolve the misalignment with a real solution, not just by delaying the pain.

RULES OF ELEVATION

In both natural and man-made goal conflicts, there is always the option to elevate the goal conflict to a level above you. This alternative should be used after trying to resolve the conflict, not as your go-to first step.

Note that elevation is different from asking for advice or giving a heads up. Asking your boss for advice on tackling a goal alignment issue makes sense regardless of the situation. Giving a heads up to your boss might also make sense if he or she is going to hear about it or be asked about the conversation. If you are approaching a person in your matrix or on your team, you may want to pull in their supervisor, depending on your relationship with both players and the nature of the issue. They may be able to advise you, clarify things, or you may need them to reinforce the message after the discussion.

Elevation takes things a step further and really lays the issue in another person's lap—like Janet's option to bring the conflict with Kenneth to her boss. You don't want to overplay this card—the risk is two-fold. First, you risk perceptions of dependence—not being willing or able to resolve things on your own. Second, you could be accused of over-dramatizing the situation. The more you elevate problems, the less potent elevation becomes and the more you look powerless.

In a matrix role, it may also be unclear whom to elevate a conflict to. It could be your boss, a team member's boss, a stakeholder's boss or all of the above. It could be the boss who sits where the matrix merges. One of the leaders I interviewed called this person "The Lowest Common Boss." Depending on how high up you have to go to find this person, he or she may be an option, but if the Lowest Common Boss is more than two levels above you, think twice.

Regardless of whom you elevate to, when you elevate, you need to have the full picture—not just your piece of the picture. The minute you elevate with just one side of the story, you have lost all credibility. Go back to your mindset—it's bigger than you.

Elevate with the full picture, not just your perspective.

ZOOM OUT

A few tips on elevating a goal conflict:

Don't ever cry wolf. Make sure you have done your homework and you have all the facts pointing to a misalignment. Don't send the person you are elevating to on a wild goose chase for a misalignment that doesn't exist.

Be objective. Present the misalignment from both sides.

Frame it in a larger context. Describe the misalignment in a larger context—not how it affects you, but how it affects team and organizational goals.

Provide your ideas on steps to resolution. Do not just place the problem in their lap, have a proposal for what to do next and all the information needed to take that next step.

A NOTE ON GOAL ALIGNMENT AND REWARDS

As you will recall from the Introduction, there are a few showstoppers in matrix roles, and one is reward. Goals are usually connected to rewards. If you are up against a competing goal with a reward linked to it that is bigger than the reward linked to yours, realize that you are limited in what you can make happen. These types of conflicts have to be brought to light—the project is set up to fail, and you will have to be unrelenting in drawing attention to this disconnect.

"Conflict is the gadfly of thought. It stirs us to observation and memory. It instigates to invention. It shocks us out of sheeplike passivity and sets us at noting and contriving."

JOHN DEWEY

The same is true if you feel a personal pull based on rewards. There will absolutely be times when goals conflict, you are stuck in the middle and the goal initiated from the side of the matrix that pays you will feel like the stronger pull. Again, these types of conflicts have to be brought to light—you are in a no-win situation and have to be unrelenting in drawing attention to this disconnect.

Alignment is a point in time. You have it momentarily, and you fight for it continuously. Like every Essential in this book, alignment doesn't grow organically, it is not natural and it needs tending. Goal misalignment is one of the biggest time wasters in matrix roles. Being good at preventing, anticipating and resolving goal conflicts frees up your time and your team's time to work constructively toward milestones. Resolving misalignments with your bosses will makes your life easier and ensure that your efforts are exerted in the correct direction, not wasted.

IN SUMMARY

EMBRACE

➔ Goal conflicts as an intended consequence of the matrix and leverage this to get optimal solutions.

➔ Your responsibility to prevent man-made conflicts—don't let goals drift and shift

➔ Inclusive goal setting to drive alignment from the beginning

➔ Vigilance in looking for misalignments and tackling them when it makes sense

TRY

➔ Get brutal with selecting goals by evaluating and stacking them against each other

➔ Once goals are set, keep them visible and use them as a framework for meetings and to prioritize work

➔ Be on the hunt for misalignments, have a forum for identifying and resolving goal conflicts

➔ When you identify a misalignment, pause long enough to ask questions and understand the nature of the issue before you either pursue both goals or resolve the conflict

➔ Follow the ground rules for matrix goal alignment: always go back to the bigger picture goal; be realistic in when you can pursue dual goals; be ready to make trade-offs and assume nothing about your partners' understanding of and engagement in your goals

IN PRACTICE

REPORTING RELATIONSHIP MATRIX

It is very likely that your bosses will have conflicting goals, with you stuck in the middle of them. Do not try to please both. Do a good job triaging, and for critical misalignments bring your bosses together and shine a spotlight on the conflict. Follow the guidelines for elevation. Things can get political. In these cases, stay neutral and do what you can to set up discussion between the two of them with the bigger organizational goal in mind.

CUSTOMER HUB MATRIX

Managing conflicting goals for you will be an almost daily occurrence, as the formally set goals of those in your hub trickle down to day-to-day priorities that conflict with your own. Aligning and inclusive goal setting are going to be absolutely critical for you. Include them in your goal setting, but also insert yourself into theirs to build your understanding and appreciation of their objectives (as well as to give input).

CROSS-FUNCTIONAL AND PROJECT TEAM MATRICES

Natural misalignments are the cornerstone of your matrix team. Don't let them frustrate you or derail the team. This is why the team exists. Get good at leveraging these conflicts by not personalizing them. Be a role model and encourage the behaviors described in the section on channeling and cultivating natural misalignments.

ESSENTIAL #3
CLARIFY ROLES

WHAT IT IS

Boundaries can blur in matrix roles. The key to understanding roles is to define them without expecting total clarity, then get comfortable with what isn't clear. Accept roles as they are; build trust to fill gaps in clarity.

WHAT YOU WILL LEARN

- » Getting things right from the start: defining roles
- » Three simple guidelines to use role clarity tools
- » Dealing with boundary breach
- » Partnership-driven resolution for role conflicts

DON is a director of Finance for a technology company. His matrix role is best described as an internal customer hub. He is the lead Finance person for a small business unit and acts as a general contractor—he is the point person for the business with a dotted line to Angel, the General Manager. He relies on a web of specialists in the Finance function to deliver on client needs.

When I asked him about role clarity, he told me a story about Diana, one of the specialists in his web. The two started their roles at the same time with a collegial relationship, but it was quickly turning hostile.

Diana seemed to throw information, requests and work products "over the fence" without much consultation with Don. Often she would have conversations with Angel that would conflict with or dilute messages that Don had delivered. For Don's part, he admitted that he often left Diana "out of the loop" because she was in a building across the campus. Sometimes he felt like he didn't have time to fill her in on what was happening with the client.

This could have continued, with each infraction fortifying the walls of their individual silos, while Angel and his team paid the price. But Don did something that I found matrix masters do a lot of. He took a step back to diagnose the problem and figure out what was within his control to address. Don had felt for some time that their roles could be clearer. What he didn't know was that this lack of role clarity was leading to behaviors that were eroding trust between the two of them.

The division was preparing for the annual budgeting process. It was an intense, highly visible, three-month process for the division, and Diana was Don's partner. Don knew the relationship with Diana was on a crash course, and the partnership required for the initiative could be the breaking point for them.

He suggested that he and Diana work together to define each task in the budgeting process and identify who would do what for each task—who would take the lead, who would provide input and what they needed to keep each other informed of. They completed this outline and shared it with Angel so he knew what to expect from each of them.

They followed the role outline for the next three months with very few issues. They referred back to it on occasion to make sure they were on track and clear on their responsibilities. The process went smoothly—hand-offs were made, each stepped up when they needed to and stepped back when it was appropriate.

As a by-product of using this structured approach to defining their roles, trust between Diana and Don increased. Because expectations were clear, there was no more "throwing things over the wall"—Diana knew when to consult Don and vice-versa. Because communication needs were unambiguous, they both felt well informed, which in turn helped them to rebuild trust. The success of this process helped make day-to-day tasks, which didn't have full, formal role documentation, much less taxing.

Don estimated it took three hours to create the role document. I asked him how much time it saved, and he responded, "Immeasurable, because it didn't just save me time on this project, it saved me time and energy on all subsequent work I did with Diana. The work flows easily now, and the increased trust allowed us to move much, much faster."

The reasons behind Don and Diana's frustrations are typical in matrix roles, as are the ramifications. In matrix roles, interdependencies increase and can become a web of converging, diverging and parallel roles. Understanding who occupies this web and what their roles are is central to getting results.

In researching this book, I asked people what they thought was most difficult about matrix roles. Over a third of their top challenges tied back to role clarity. For example, accountability was often mentioned. When roles aren't defined, holding people accountable is like nailing Jell-O to a wall. Decision-making was also a high-ranking item. When it is unclear who should be involved or what rights they have, decision-making is painfully slow. Power struggles, another frequently cited impediment, also regularly result from lack of role clarity, overlaid with a fair amount of ego. Lack of role clarity is at the root of the biggest challenges in the matrix and a major contributor to the ambiguity that afflicts matrix roles.

> Holding people accountable, decision-making and power struggles were all identified as top challenges. All can be traced back to issues of role clarity.
>
> ✓ SURVEY

Organizational charts, job titles and job descriptions are all great starting points for role clarity, but they certainly don't provide the full picture of a dynamic matrix role. Assumptions and misunderstandings happen in matrix roles because you are working without lane markers. As one interviewee described to me, "At the start of the year, the starting gun goes off, and you begin the race toward your goal. You may start in your own lane, but pretty soon everyone is focused on the finish line, not on their lane or who they are bumping into on their way down the track."

There will always be questions about "who does what" in a matrix—there is no way to thoroughly and conclusively define roles in organizations as dynamic as these. A little investment in defining roles upfront can provide a framework, and trust will help smooth out the rough edges. When the inevitable boundary breach comes up, dealing with it in the right way can not only resolve the conflict but strengthen the partnership.

GETTING THINGS RIGHT FROM THE START—DEFINING ROLES

For key partners, decisions or tasks, an investment in deliberate role definition can make a huge difference in getting things done effectively and efficiently and building a partnership. Don realized this as his relationship with Diana started to settle into the Dysfunctional Partner level.

The most widely used method for detailed role defining, called a RACI chart, outlines who is **R**esponsible, **A**ccountable, **C**onsulted or **I**nformed on a task or decision. RAPID (**R**esponsible, **A**ccountable, **P**erform, **I**nform, **De**cide) and RASCI (**R**esponsible, **A**ccountable, **S**upporting, **C**onsulted, **I**nformed) are also variations.

For the Budget Planning Process, Don and Diana's chart may have looked something like this:

		RESPONSIBLE: Responsible for completing a work product	**ACCOUNTABLE:** Ensures this task is completed	**CONSULT:** Gives input into how task is carried out or into work product	**INFORM:** Kept apprised of progress and outcome
DECISIONS/TASKS	Working with cost center managers to complete budget paperwork	Don	Bob (corporate process owner)	Angel	Diana
	Producing budget planning reports	Don	Bob (corporate process owner)	Diana	Angel
	Planning agenda and logistics for budget review meeting	Diana	Nancy (Diana's boss)	Don	Angel
	Facilitating budget review meeting	Diana	Nancy (Diana's boss)	Don	Bob (corporate process owner)
	Finalizing budget reports	Don	Bob (corporate process owner)	Diana	Angel
	Sharing meeting output with cost center managers	Angel's management team	Angel	Don	Diana

This approach steers you toward defining roles at ground level instead of at 30,000 feet. For Don and Diana, the high-altitude distinction of "General Contractor" and "Specialist" wasn't enough. It wasn't until they talked about roles within a specific process (the budget planning process) and used a RACI tool that they reached a functional level of detail on their responsibilities.

The chart is a handy tool for moving quickly through action planning and decision-making. It can serve as an accountability mechanism and can be a safe starting place for conversations about role clarity. It positions the conversation as a discussion of what is happening vis-à-vis the outline, not your personal opinion. As one interviewee put it, "I use the RACI chart because when it comes to holding someone accountable for playing a specific role, the chart becomes the bad guy, not me."

> *"Perfect clarity would profit the intellect but damage the will."*
>
> BLAISE PASCAL

The discussions that go into constructing a RACI-type chart are often as beneficial as the chart itself. They force a team or partnership to be very precise about the tasks and decisions in front of them and where and how they overlap and connect. This process promotes conversations that may not happen otherwise.

Because the dialogue that goes into creating the role document is so rich, bring as many people as is practical into this process. For a reporting relationship matrix, include both bosses and bring in the employee to review the document. For teams, bring the full team together to discuss and include their bosses in a review discussion. The closer people are to the construction of this plan and the more opportunity they have to ask questions, the better your product and their understanding will be.

> Bring as many people in on role clarity discussions as practical; being part of the process adds to understanding and ownership of the role definitions.
>
> ZOOM OUT

Whether your role definition is high level or as detailed as a RACI chart, test for clarity and agreement by running it through some "what if" scenarios with your team or partner, or maybe even garner outside opinions. For example, Don and Diana could have posed scenarios such as:

- What if one of us gets a question that is part of the other's role?
- Will a shift in timelines change the roles at all?
- How do we use each other's "input"? When do we need it, and when do we make the call ourselves?
- What if we reach an impasse on a decision we need to make?

Whatever shape your role definition takes, make sure it is documented and accessible. Role clarity in matrix roles really never ends. It needs focus and consistent (if not constant) tending. Roles shift over time or reveal themselves differently based on the specific task or project, so updating this knowledge is key.

THREE SIMPLE GUIDELINES FOR USING ROLE CLARITY TOOLS

Role clarity is a noble endeavor, but implemented incorrectly or for the wrong reasons, it can be damaging. This was painfully obvious for a client I worked with who had recently implemented a role definition guide for their product development teams. This story illustrates what can go wrong when you insert structured role clarity into an organization whose real issue is trust.

The organization was a US subsidiary of a large European company. They invested significant organizational resources on an initiative intended to clarify roles for roughly 10 different types of project team members using a RACI-type model. The final role document filled a two-inch binder. Six months after implementing this initiative, they asked me to conduct post-mortem interviews with project team members to answer two questions: Were people using the role outline? Was the framework helping teams work more efficiently?

I interviewed project team members and learned that the binder *was* being used…as a weapon. The minute someone even looked like they might be stepping outside their role, another team member pounced, using the role document as support. When asked if it was used proactively in planning who would do what on a certain task, the response typically was, "No, more for lining up evidence of an infraction."

Margaret was the vice president of one of the functions that was represented on the team, and she was especially critical of the role definitions. She told me about Sean, a relatively new project manager who carried the binder around with him everywhere—passages highlighted, pages tabbed for easy reference. He was particularly keen on pointing out offenses committed by Margaret's team, which made Margaret and her team extremely defensive and mistrustful of him. This mistrust made them resist his efforts to enforce the guidelines of the document and sent them on a quest to identify *his* encroachments.

Sean was the extreme, but not the exception. It became obvious through my conversations that many team members were gripping on to that role definition binder like it was their only floatation device in the middle of the ocean. For Sean, and I suspect for others, this was killing his trustworthiness and credibility. In his singular focus on roles, he was losing sight of his own role—to make the project successful, specifically by bringing a new product to market.

It was also apparent that not only was the organization fixing the wrong problem, but their solution was actually making the real problem worse. Roles may not have been crystal clear, but the bigger issue was trust. Would teams that trusted each other need roles documented at this level of detail? Teams with high trust tend to move in and out of roles fluidly, not taking much offense if liberties are taken with how roles are carried out.

Finally, the teams were using the role definitions as a way to substantiate claims of boundary breach—basically using the tool against each other. These conflicts were divisive, not collaborative, and they were missing opportunities to use the role definition documents proactively in planning how they would get things done.

This story was about a large-scale organizational effort to clarify roles, but the same dynamics are involved in one-to-one situations (like Don and Diana). Keep these three guidelines in mind on your quest for role clarity.

1. Don't assume role clarity is the problem, look at trust. Role clarity can seem like an easy solution for teams and partnerships—far easier than dealing with the fact that they don't trust each other. By itself, clarification of roles won't increase trust or improve a partnership. But when coupled with genuine intent and actions to improve the partnership (like those outlined in Essential #1), role clarity can help put a relationship back on track, as in the case of Don and Diana.

2. Use role definitions offensively, not just defensively. Any role clarity mechanism runs the risk of being used as a weapon. Especially in low-trust settings, it can become a conduit for trust issues. Role definitions are best used proactively, in initial project planning and as tasks or decisions emerge, not when you are reacting to a boundary breach and emotions are high. Boundary breaches are inevitable, but there are better ways to handle them (as described later in this chapter).

3. Don't ever put it on the shelf. Role clarity is a point in time, and the outline is a living document. There will be infractions. Sometimes those infractions can lead you to an even better, clearer definition. Revise and edit accordingly.

DEALING WITH BOUNDARY BREACH

Boundary breach will happen, no matter how thorough and inclusive your process or how comprehensive your outline. Although you don't want to carry you role binder around looking for a target, there will be times when you have to confront an infraction. But before you jump in, step back and ask three questions:

» Why did it happen?
» Is it worth confronting?
» What's the best way to confront it?

WHY BOUNDARY BREACH HAPPENS

A marketing team and a team of clinical experts (made up of physicians, nurses and pharmacists) were brought into a matrix to develop and commercialize complex products used in a hospital setting. Close collaboration between the marketing team and the clinical team was critical. The collaboration was not terribly effective, and, thinking that role clarity might be the cause, the team leaders asked me to help clarify the two teams' roles. After interviewing both teams, it was clear that there were a few people who were new on the team and simply not sure where their role stopped and another's started. But the more prevalent issue was that the clinical team didn't like taking orders from marketing, and marketing didn't like having to clear everything through clinical. Well-defined roles, just nobody liked them much.

Boundary breach happens for a variety of reasons ranging from innocently unaware to deliberately defying. The explanations can be thought of as a continuum:

| They didn't know | They forgot | They misunderstood | They thought it was an exception | They don't accept it |

Starting from the left hand side of the scale, "They didn't know" or "They forgot" is entirely plausible in a matrix. Chances are, the people in your web are also part of other webs, and unless your organization is really consistent about role definition, each of these has their own unique assumptions and guidelines around roles.

"They misunderstood" and "They thought it was an exception" are both evidence of the big gray area that remains even after you do a thorough job defining roles. Misunderstandings are bound to happen, because defining a role comprehensively and definitively is impossible. There will always be room for interpretation or wording that isn't entirely clear. As mentioned earlier, there is also a difference between the understanding of people who were "in the room" when the roles were defined and those handed the final product. The latter don't have the benefit of the discussion behind the paper, which will impact their understanding.

Exceptions crop up because there will be "what if" scenarios you didn't consider. Accounting for all possible exceptions is impossible. In addition, a matrix by definition is an amalgamation of many different perspectives and areas of expertise. What looks straightforward from one point of view (and therefore calling for the action as prescribed in your role definition) may look like an exception requiring a departure from the playbook from another person's point of view.

At the far right-hand side of the scale of explanations, we reach what I call *role acceptance*—the roles are clear, but we just don't like them. It is one thing to nod your head in acceptance to an outline of responsibilities on paper. But sometimes when those roles actually play out, acceptance is not so easy.

WHEN TO TACKLE ROLE CONFLICTS

Assessing why the breach happened helps you assess the next step—choosing your course of action. Your response should be based on the nature and impact of the boundary breach, your relationship with the person and the risk involved.

> Your response should be based on the nature and impact of the boundary breach, your relationship with the person and the risk involved.
>
> **TRIAGE**

Role clarity documents are great accountability mechanisms, but they aren't laws that need constant surveillance and enforcement. Show flexibility and trust by not addressing, discussing and debriefing every little infringement. This buys you wiggle room when you step out of your own agreed-upon role.

You should let it go if this is the first time you have seen the person make a particular mistake, and it doesn't have much of an impact on your goal or the morale of the people involved. Let it go if it is truly an exception that won't come up again. Also let it go if the politics created by addressing the issue are worse than the role infraction itself.

Tackling a conflict can take different forms (as discussed in the "Partnership-driven resolution" section)—ranging from a quick discussion focused on reminding them of the content of the role document to a conflict resolution discussion.

Here's when you want to approach people. In a clear case of misinformation or misunderstanding—don't miss the opportunity to refer them back to the role outline. When a trend becomes evident, with repeated infringements from the same person or on the same task, discuss it. If the behavior sets a precedent and permanently moves role markers, talk about it. And finally, you must confront if the behavior negatively impacts milestones, work product or team morale.

PARTNERSHIP-DRIVEN RESOLUTION FOR ROLE CONFLICTS

When you have decided to tackle the boundary issue, a little planning is called for because the person you are approaching most likely is or should be a partner. Let's go back to the possible explanations for the boundary breach to determine your course of action:

Not surprisingly, the explanations on the left-hand side have one necessary action—reiterate the roles. A simple, "Hey by the way just wanted to remind/let you know" conversation is warranted.

As you move toward the middle, reiteration is still needed, but so is refining. Misunderstandings and exceptions should cause you to consider refining role definitions. "Hey by the way" might be followed with, "let's take a look at how we can tweak the role outline to make sure it is clearer and more useful for us."

In the case of lack of acceptance, or when there is a trend for repeated missteps by the same person, a number of carefully delivered messages are necessary. You will need to reiterate, potentially go as far as renegotiating roles and recognize that accepting the role may be difficult. Clearly, these are the trickiest circumstances. The first key is to walk in assuming it *is* one of the other circumstances. We tend to see our own boundary breaches as accidents or attempts to "help out," but see others as overstepping their bounds and encroaching on our territory. If you grant their intentions the same leniency that you

Do not assume they are rejecting the role as defined. Assume clarity is at issue.

MINDSET

grant you own, you will walk in assuming best intent—which sets the tone for the interaction.

After a shift to "best intent" mindset, you will need to think about your message and your words. Here's how I might coach Don and Diana, our Finance friends from earlier, on confronting each other on role acceptance.

	SAY THIS ...	NOT THAT ...
START WITH A SAFE OPENING	"I wanted to circle back on the role agreements we set up last month…"	"I am here to talk to you about not following the commitments we laid out in the role document."
KEEP IT TENTATIVE AND REITERATE	"We had agreed that you would complete the paperwork and keep me informed, but I haven't heard anything from you on it. Maybe I missed an email from you?"	"Even though we agreed you would complete the paperwork and keep me informed, so far you have done nothing to keep me in the loop."
RECOGNIZE IT MAY BE TOUGH TO ACCEPT	"I know it must be frustrating having me in the middle of this with you and Angel, but I do think keeping me updated will help us better manage this consistently."	"You have to accept that I am involved in this, and it's not just you and Angel running this initiative."
RENEGOTIATE	"Would it make more sense for us to just set up 30-minute calls each week, than to leave it impromptu?"	"You agreed to it, so you need to stick to it."

The difference between these two columns is significant. On the right you have a forceful and compliance-driven tone. The left is unassuming and aiming for agreement and ownership. In a matrix role, you don't have the authority to force compliance; your approach will need to focus not only on resolution but building the partnership.

> In a matrix role, you don't have the authority to force compliance; your approach will need to focus not only on resolution but building the partnership.
>
> JUJITSU

These words may seem too soft for you, or not sound like you—that's OK. It isn't necessary to use them verbatim. You need to find your own style and way of positioning things. Just walking in assuming best intent, being tentative, asking questions and recognizing the difficulty of the situation will be huge trust builders.

The approach in this section assumes you have some sort of outline of roles. Agreed-upon role outlines are a powerful, objective starting point for these discussions. Without one, you have no basis for your claim, no point of reference, and you may even have to overcome judgments on why you are questioning their actions. Even if you don't do a full formal RACI chart, some sort of structured dialogue is vital to holding people accountable in matrix roles. It should outline roles around tasks and decisions and be documented and accessible.

LAST RESORT: ELEVATE IT

Any role conflict has the potential to be sticky. Some are stickier than others. Although you don't want to overplay this card, there are times when you will need to pull in help to tackle a role issue. Issues involving acceptance can fall into this category. Acceptance often starts at the top. Remember the marketing and clinical teams that couldn't work together? Do you know who resisted those roles more than anyone? The leaders—there were disagreements on roles at the very top of the business unit, and they trickled down through the organization.

"It takes generosity to discover the whole through others. If you realize you are only a violin, you can open yourself up to the world by playing your role in the concert."

JACQUES YVES COUSTEAU

When the conflict is bigger than you—the infraction is a result of disconnects at a higher level—you will want to consider elevating it. If you have repeatedly approached the person on a role misstep and the behavior persists, you should elevate it. The same Rules of Elevation outlined in Essential #2 apply here.

When done well, bringing others in can be a powerful tool in resolving any type of conflict. Overplayed, it may send the wrong messages to your boss(es) and team. Use it sparingly and effectively on the trickiest of role conflicts.

You'll never eliminate the ambiguity of matrix roles. There is a limit to how much a role can be defined, so you need to clarify what you can and get comfortable with the ambiguity that remains. Very few roles are unambiguous, and those that are would probably bore you to tears. Get used to it. Better yet, get good at it. Whether defining your role versus others in your web or keeping the roles of multiple bosses straight, role clarity is a journey, not a destination. Trying to completely eliminate ambiguity will just exhaust you and take your focus off your goals. The good news is that this ambiguity also holds the opportunity to shape your own role. If you embrace the freedom that ambiguity provides, you will find opportunities to try things outside of your box. Few people are motivated by ambiguity, but some are challenged by it and thrive in this type of environment. Be one of those people.

IN SUMMARY

EMBRACE

➔ The fact that the nature of matrix roles means boundaries are blurred; get used to having your toes stepped on and stepping on other's

➔ The need to be proactive in defining roles, but realistic in what role clarity can provide

➔ Tackling the critical role conflicts in a partnership-driven way

TRY

➔ Be as inclusive as possible when defining roles. If you are working with a team, consider bringing their direct bosses in as reviewers. Having them in the same room builds understanding and reinforces their role in making the person and the project successful

➔ Use your role descriptors as tasks come up, not just on front-end planning. At the end of a meeting, run your team's to-do list through the role descriptors to make sure marching orders are clear. This reinforces the use of the tool and ensures consistency in how you label different roles.

➔ Check in on role outlines—make changes, add details, ask others to review them.

➔ Make sure role documents are user-friendly and accessible (on a shared drive, collaboration site, etc.)

➔ When you are considering whether to confront a boundary breach, work through the situation with someone who isn't involved—they will be more objective about whether it is a breach big enough and important enough to confront.

IN PRACTICE

REPORTING RELATIONSHIP MATRIX

The role conflict that is prevalent here is between your two bosses—who do you turn to for what? Answering this question actually starts with another question: "Why is the extra reporting relationship needed? What is it expected to bring?" The answer should be stated in terms of what it brings to the organization, as well as what it brings to the individual. Once the stake is in the ground on what you want to accomplish and why, you will need to settle on who takes the lead and what their roles are in not only specific tasks and projects but also in managing and coaching you.

CUSTOMER HUB MATRIX

The bounty of handoffs in a Customer Hub Matrix makes role clarity at the task level critical. A RACI-type definition is needed and may need to be done to a fairly minute level with critical tasks or customers. Especially sensitive is the communication to the customer. Although those in a hub shouldn't be sequestered from the customer, chances are the customer will prefer one "point of contact." Get specific when you are defining who interfaces with the customer and when.

CROSS-FUNCTIONAL AND PROJECT TEAM MATRICES

Bring direct bosses into the team's role clarity discussions. Having them in the same room builds understanding and reinforces their role in making the person and the project successful. Role definitions and task assignments that are made in a team meeting may make perfect sense, but will they stand up to the test of the real world when bosses start to ask questions and influence what has been defined? Get them involved to pressure-test the role definition and to get their buy-in.

"It is not always what we know or analyzed before we make a decision that makes it a great decision. It is what we do after we make the decision to implement and execute it that makes it a good decision."

WILLIAM POLLARD

ESSENTIAL #4

GET DECISIONS MADE

WHAT IT IS

The decisions in matrix roles, like the matrix structure itself, bring together diverse perspectives, divergent agendas and priorities, and competing interests. Decisions tend to be complex, and there are high expectations for transparency and inclusion. You leverage partnerships, align goals and clarify roles. You bring to bear your influence, communication and meeting leadership skills.

WHAT YOU WILL LEARN

» The key differences between decision-making in traditional roles and matrix roles
» Five rules for getting decisions made in a matrix role

VICTORIA

VICTORIA was a surgeon at a large teaching hospital. She had just moved into an administrative role leading a large project that would enable the hospital to go paperless—essentially a project team matrix. As a surgeon, her decision-making rights and authority were crystal clear. But her new job, which required her to straddle several different matrices, was high on inclusion and consensus. Not unexpectedly, no one warned her of this or coached her on how her approach needed to change. She came in and did what she had always done—made decisions, told people what those decisions were and expected that they would carry things out. She started getting questions about the "why" behind her decisions. She perceived this as questioning of her judgment and responded by digging in her heels. She wasn't about to set a precedent for going back on decisions she had made. She was also questioned about "how" she made a decision, which completely confounded her—how did she make a decision? With her 25 years of experience, of course! How could one possibly break down into steps what just came naturally to her after seeing it all before?

The questions—while frustrating, annoying and just plain time-consuming—she could probably live with. What she couldn't live with was seeing that her decisions weren't being implemented. It was like people were ignoring her. Not only did they not follow her directives, they were downright resistant, and eventually a revolt began to brew. When given the feedback that she was running roughshod over people and they weren't appreciating it, her response was, "I am just getting stuff done—isn't that what I am being paid for?"

KEY DIFFERENCES BETWEEN DECISION-MAKING IN TRADITIONAL AND MATRIX ROLES

Decision-making in a traditional role is like running a quarter-mile race around a track—clear start and finish, clear lanes. Getting decisions made in a matrix role is an obstacle course. It requires you to sprint, slow down, jump, crawl, zig and zag. If you go into a decision in a matrix role by training, thinking and running like it is a race around a track, you will frustrate yourself and those around you and most likely not reach the finish line. That's probably why over 70% of the people surveyed for this book listed getting decisions made, figuring out who the decision maker is and including the right people as top challenges in matrix roles.

Over 70% of the people surveyed for this book listed getting decisions made, figuring out who the decision maker is and including the right people as top challenges in matrix roles.

SURVEY

Victoria was the star of the quarter-mile sprint in her role as a surgeon. But because no one told her that the track was now an obstacle course, she continued to sprint, plowing right through the obstacles. There are definitely times when plowing down is called for—but it's probably not when you join a new team, and it can't serve as your primary strategy in a matrix role. For Victoria, employing this strategy early and often was resulting in diminishing returns. Here are a few of the key distinctions she and others miss:

	TRADITIONAL ROLES / ORGANIZATIONS	MATRIX ROLES/ ORGANIZATIONS
MAKING THE DECISION	Hierarchy/title-driven Straightforward, linear Often behind closed doors, unstructured Often exclusive	Expertise, role, input-driven Complex, much back and forth Need for transparent process Inclusive
EXECUTING THE DECISION	Authority-driven Communication on the "what" of the decision Requires little follow-up	Ownership-driven Communication is transparent on the what, why, how and who Can require significant follow-up
KEY CHALLENGES	Making the right decision and using authority to implement	Balancing decision-making speed with inclusion Knowing who is the ultimate decision-maker Gaining ownership in the decision to make it "stick"

FIVE RULES FOR GETTING DECISIONS MADE IN A MATRIX ROLE

As one of my interviewees put it, "decision-making in a matrix is less about 'making' and more about 'finessing.'" This "finessing" requires adherence to five rules:

Decision-making in a matrix requires more give and take, more finesse than force.

JUJITSU

Rule #1: Balance and toggle your decision-making styles

Rule #2: Watch your biases

Rule #3: Set it up right

Rule #4: Invest in agreement

Rule #5: Go the extra mile to make sure the decision sticks

RULE #1: BALANCE AND TOGGLE YOUR DECISION-MAKING STYLES

The bane of Victoria's existence in her new role was the seemingly endless number of people who had input, interest or pure curiosity into her decisions and decision-making process. She did what many people in matrix roles do—she reacted to others' need for inclusion and information by drawing more distinct lines in her sandbox. She let fewer and fewer people in and became less forthcoming about her decisions and decision-making process. What she may have gained in the speed of decision-making, she was losing on the implementation end because of the lack of ownership that exclusive decision-making can create.

For people like Victoria who are used to calling the shots, the inclusion-based nature of matrix decision-making is the biggest and most critical adjustment you must make to be successful. Even when a decision appears to be yours and yours alone, chances are the decision will be better if you get input from others, and chances are you will need others to make your decision happen. Simply put: input in making the decision makes the decision better and builds ownership in the implementation. Both of these are critical given how interwoven most decisions are, and how much you will need to rely on influence vs. authority to make decisions happen.

> Even when a decision appears to be yours and yours alone, chances are the decision will be better if you get input from others, and chances are you will need others to make your decision stick.
>
> **MINDSET**

Victoria represents one end of the spectrum. Now meet Marcus—Victoria's polar opposite. Marcus was a quality manager for a manufacturing company, with a dual-reporting relationship with the head of Quality and the plant manager at his site. He included everyone on everything. Even for the smallest decisions, he brought in both bosses. He didn't want to discount one or the other, wanted to make sure all three of them were in agreement. At his year-end performance review, the bosses raised the white flag. They could no longer take the over-inclusion and the time it was consuming. "Just do it!" they implored.

The consensus Marcus sought wasn't ill intended, just ill placed. Consensus (seeking the best possible decision that all stakeholders can live with) is an important strategy in matrix decision-making. But it is overused, and because it is overused, it gets a bad rap. We tend to swing from being self-appointed sheriffs (Victoria) to camp counselors trying to get everyone to sing Kumbaya over every decision (Marcus). Good matrix managers balance the need for speed with the need for inclusion and by doing this, toggle between various decision-making styles.

There are several options for your matrix decision-making approach. But in a matrix role, a couple of things are not options. The first is getting input. Given the complex interwoven nature of the problems and solutions, input is required in nearly every matrix decision. Broad-based involvement in implementation is also not optional—many decisions will be bigger than your area of responsibility, and you will have to reach out to give a decision arms and legs. But what lies in the middle is where you can (and must) expand and contract—it's

For input and implementation of decisions, you must look broadly at who to bring in.

ZOOM OUT

how the decision is actually made. Most effective matrix decision-making processes look something like this:

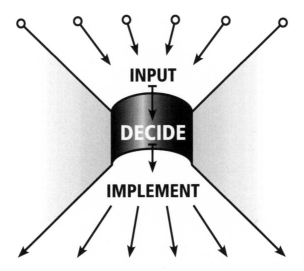

The center of this flow of input and implementation—the actual activity of deciding—can and should grow and shrink based on the decision. Even graphically it is balanced and stable. Compare this to what Victoria's approach might look like in visual form:

For her, not only did the center shrink, so did the top and bottom of the funnel, leaving her with a decision with very little stability and staying power. This approach works fine with a decision that only affects you and only requires you to implement—but those are rare in a matrix role. Even if Victoria didn't bring others in on the decision-making, she would have been better served by investing in a broader reach for implementation to give things a bit of stability:

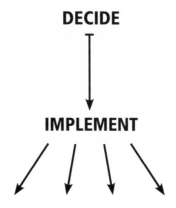

If we drew Marcus' decision-making approach, it would resemble a square—he involved everyone in each phase:

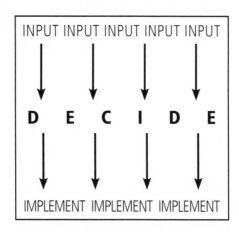

Although the visual makes it appear balanced and stable, the investment is just not worth it. It's like calling in the SWAT team to rescue a kitten in a tree. The investment is neither practical nor neccessary.

Matrix mastery requires you to toggle between different decision-making strategies—to grow and shrink that center portion as it fits the decision and to provide reinforcement by bringing others into the process. It also means knowing when your decision-making approach isn't working and you need a

Plan B. For example, if you are going for group consensus and get stuck, you should move to a single decision maker—more on that later in the chapter.

If you are like Marcus, the narrowing point of matrix decision-making often proves troublesome, because it ruffles feathers. No one wants to make the call on who's in and who's out. Alternatively, if roles aren't clear, we truly can't put our finger on who the decision maker is or who should be included. Both scenarios lead to the same result: we let everyone in on the decision, and decision-making grinds to a halt.

Knowing whom to pull in when is the key to balancing inclusion with speed and toggling between different decision-making approaches. You have to narrow at some point. Having clear roles helps (Essential #3), as do these considerations:

Those who:

» must buy into the decision

» have the information, expertise or experience

INPUT

DECIDE

Shrinks or expands based on level of:

» buy-in required to implement

» time investment warranted or available

» complexity of decision

IMPLEMENT

Those who:

» must take specific action based on the decision

» influence those who must take specific action

» will be affected by the decision

At each step, transparency is key. People need to know why you are including them or not including them. Be upfront about this process (giving input is different from being part of the decision-making group). There will always be people who want to be included but aren't. Be forthcoming with this as well.

RULE #2: WATCH YOUR BIASES

Many, many biases cloud our decision-making process. The Recency Effect says we tend to place more importance on information or events that we experience most recently. The Primacy Effect occurs when we put more weight on events or information we hear first. If we are subject to Confirmation Bias, we search for or interpret information that confirms our opinion. With Distinction Bias, we may view two options as more dissimilar when evaluating them simultaneously than when evaluating them separately. If you read this and think you don't have biases, or at least not as many as others do, then you just fell into the Bias Blind Spot—the tendency to see oneself as less biased than other people.

Biases are natural to human behavior and can't be completely eliminated. The fact that groups function more often as the decision-making bodies in matrix organizations helps allay some of this—group members can balance each other's biases or call them out. However, each matrix role can add a unique set of biases to beware of:

MATRIX ROLE	MATRIX BIAS
Reporting Relationship	Align more closely with one boss versus another based on common function, geography, exposure or style.
Customer Hub	Align so vehemently with a customer that it impacts ability to understand and appreciate the perspective/needs of the internal matrix
Project Team	Align so vehemently with a project that it impacts ability to understand and appreciate the perspective/needs of the functions represented on the team
Cross-functional Team	Put more weight on information from your own functional area because of your understanding and familiarity with it

You need to be doubly diligent in watching for bias in matrix decision-making. Not only must you watch for common decision biases but matrix-specific biases. Bias can hamper your ability to get the right people involved, get the full picture of the considerations and implications of a decision and implement fully and effectively.

RULE #3: SET IT UP RIGHT

A route that you have driven many times becomes rote, subconscious, automatic. Drive the same route with someone following you who has never driven it before, and your approach will be very different. You lay out your route with them prior to leaving, slow down, check your mirror and put your blinker on earlier. You invest more effort both before and during your journey to get you both there safely.

Decision-making in matrix roles is a bit like that. It is very conscious, very structured and planned out—there must be upfront investment. You need to plan things out and check in frequently to make sure everyone is still with you. When you are taking others along for the ride, there has to be a well-defined process that starts at the moment you realize a decision needs to be made and continues until the decision is thoroughly implemented or embedded in the organization.

Here are the general elements for setting up a decision:

Name it: It sounds simple, but a good decision-making process starts by recognizing that there is a decision on the table and labeling it. "OK, we have a decision here—do we want to limit the review period to two days or extend to four?" Calling this out defines the start of the process and is also a great way to check that everyone agrees that this is indeed the decision on the table. For instance, in this example, the decision very well could be whether there should be a limit on review time at all. A subtle difference, but the frame shifts how you will make the decision. When I ask leaders or leadership teams to describe decisions they have made in the past month, I am generally met with blank stares. Teams struggle to articulate decisions, and leaders are caught flat-footed. The optimist in me wants to believe decision-making is such a natural part of what they do that describing it is like asking someone to describe that last breath they took. The realist in me believes we do a lousy job labeling decisions and initiating the decision-making process. Why is this important in matrix roles? Because in matrix roles, you are bringing others with you along the way—to get input, define options, make the decision, communicate the decision and execute the decision. You can't do any of that unless you say, "This is the decision we have to make." You must lay it on the table.

Label it: Remember our discussion earlier in the chapter about Victoria and Marcus' decision-making approaches and the options you have? It can be group input with a singular decision maker, consensus or consensus with a fallback (work toward consensus for a defined period of time and if consensus is not reached, it defaults to a decision by a specific, named person). Let people know which it is. Nothing is more frustrating than thinking you are part of the decision-making process only to find that you have input but aren't a decision maker. Remember, people tend to have high inclusion needs and assumptions in matrix roles. If and how you are including them needs to be transparent so that they understand what is expected of them and can participate appropriately.

Set the criteria: Without criteria, decision-making can go on endlessly—especially in a matrix, where individual criteria can usurp collective criteria and get in the way of the ever-present trade-offs required. Set the criteria (again, the more inclusive, the better) and keep them front and center for all those involved in decision-making. The criteria you use will also facilitate implementation—people are more likely to accept a decision that went through a vigorous criteria-based process. And they will always want to know the "why" behind a decision. These natural tendencies are even stronger in a matrix organization because those on the receiving end are being asked to do something, stop doing something or change the way they are doing something by someone who most likely doesn't have direct authority over them.

Because matrix decisions attempt to bring together multiple diverse perspectives, personalities and needs, they require diligent set-up. While the set-up may seem like it is taking up time, the investment in time helps you pick up speed in reaching agreement by getting everyone working on the same page. It saves time in implementation, as you will get fewer questions when those implementing understand and respect the process that was followed. Not to mention, your decision quality can be improved by employing an objective, methodical process.

RULE #4: INVEST IN AGREEMENT

I was working with a company on an initiative to change their culture. They had outlined a number of key behaviors they wanted instilled into the culture, including two that were critical: supporting team decisions in word and deed, and open debate. At first we struggled because these behaviors seemed to be in opposition—one was supportive and the other required questioning and challenging. But the more we talked, the more we realized that supporting team decisions was entirely dependent on the opportunity to debate them. People found it difficult to support team decisions if they weren't engaged in debate at some point in the process, and their commitments carried less weight without debate. What's more, after discussing this, we also realized another piece of the company culture—continually "re-making" decisions—was caused by the same issue. Decisions were re-opened because people either weren't engaged or didn't feel heard in the initial decision-making phase. The organization wasn't investing in agreement, and they were paying a price in implementation as well as in the quality of the decision.

If you have ever observed a team reaching agreement, you know how unsightly it can be. The process can be difficult. Behind every well thought-out, effectively implemented decision is a progression of back and forth and up and down that shouldn't be short-circuited. My writing coach, Wally Bock, explained the difference between a good chapter and a great chapter by comparing it to microwaved food and conventionally cooked food—"Microwaved food doesn't taste as good because it didn't go through the process." The same can be said of decisions. Reaching agreement isn't about shortcutting the process—we can't microwave it. At the same time, you can't stay in the process forever—to continue the cooking analogy, you don't want to boil everything down to mush. It's about making investments in the process to make it more focused and efficient.

Decision-making starts by following Rules 1–3. It should involve a handful of key decision makers who are deputized to make the decision—not stand-ins, not representatives, but real decision makers—unfettered by bias and working on a clearly laid out decision, process and criteria.

After that, the dialogue kicks in, your investment in agreement begins, and your role as facilitator is in high gear. Here are a few keys to going through the process but not getting mired in it.

Use meetings: A well-run meeting (as described in Essential #7) is to decision-making what a great set of tires is to a racecar. Meetings give you speed, traction and stability when you are seeking to reach agreement. To do it well, you must think through the sequence of review, analysis and discussion that is necessary to reach concurrence. Once you lay that out, determine at which points a meeting is necessary. From there follow the steps here as well as in Essential #7.

Use white space: How you use the time before and between meetings is as important as the meetings themselves. White space is a dangerous place in matrix organizations. This is where decisions get forgotten, decision makers become distracted and your whole process can fall apart. During this time, work one-on-one with decision makers, follow up on questions and ensure they are doing their homework. Don't let the pending decision get lost in the throng of other matrix priorities.

Set a time limit and have a Plan B: Whether it is one hour or one year, set a time limit for reaching agreement and let them know what happens if you reach that limit. Does the decision get elevated to a higher-level decision maker? Do you make it? Someone else? A large-scale project leader I spoke with told me he initiated decision-making with teams with this preamble: "You can either make the decision in the next... [whatever timeframe]...or I will make it. And I assure you, I will be totally unencumbered by fact." The thought of someone else making the decision for them is usually a great motivation to work hard toward agreement.

Pull back to look at the overall objective: It is easy for people to slip back into representing only their piece of the matrix in the heat of decision-making. Periodically pull back and remind them of the bigger-picture objective. Jim, a former GM of a large business, told this wonderful story about a decision he was making with one of his matrix partners. An issue arose with a product that fell into both business units: there was a decision of which business would get the gross profit. Prior to the meeting, Jim and his team pulled together all of the facts that would support his

> Periodically pull back and remind people of the bigger-picture objective to ensure they don't fall back into their side of the matrix in the heat of decision-making.
>
> **ZOOM OUT**

division getting the gross profit. It is probably safe to assume his partner did the same. Things got heated in the meeting as both sides made their case. Finally Jim said, "This is crazy. There's only one stock price. You can take 100%. If it doesn't affect the stock price, it doesn't matter who gets it." A decision that had been argued for three months was resolved in five minutes, and Jim and his team became known as the reasonable team players.

> Sometimes giving or giving in sets the stage for influencing decisions later on.
>
> **JUJITSU**

Take a vote and ask what it would take: When you are in the middle of decision-making, occasionally go back to your criteria and, if there are options on the table, take a quick vote to see how far apart you are. Ask those in the minority what it would take to push them to another option. Most likely, you will come up with a new set of alternatives and be closer to agreement.

Use scenarios: Sometimes taking things out of the hypothetical can present new options or be the tipping point for agreement. When you are getting close to a decision, play the options out. Given the complexity of matrix decisions, you may be creating unintended consequences, and this may lead you to different options or closer to consensus. Scenarios are also helpful in checking agreement. If you have landed on a consensus decision: "We are going to extend the review period to two weeks," check agreement by asking scenario questions: "So that means that even when we have a priority project, we are going to allow the committee two weeks to review?" Simple questions like this can ensure that your agreement is solid.

Facilitating these decision-making discussions is challenging—people do this for a living. Acting as the facilitator can be tough when most likely you are also one of the decision makers and/or implementers of the decision. If it is a critical decision with sticky political angles, consider bringing in a third party. That will lend objectivity to the process and allow you to participate in the discussion.

RULE #5: GO THE EXTRA MILE TO MAKE SURE THE DECISION STICKS

The only thing tougher than getting a decision made in a matrix is getting it to stick across functions, geographies and levels. Lack of adhesion is often a symptom of the process, not the decision itself. There are three components that help ensure a decision sticks: (1) a structured, credible process, (2) including the right people in the right way and (3) consistent, transparent communication and follow-up. Here's what can happen when you are missing a piece:

A STRUCTURED, CREDIBLE PROCESS	INCLUDE THE RIGHT PEOPLE IN THE RIGHT WAY	CONSISTENT, TRANSPARENT COMMUNICATION AND FOLLOW-UP	YOU DECISION IS LIKELY TO BE:
X	X	X	Implemented and integrated
	X	X	Questioned
X		X	Overturned or ignored
X	X		Forgotten

Even if you make the right upfront investments in terms of designing and executing a strong process and involving the right people, sometimes you get tired or have moved on to the next issue come implementation time. As a result, implementation is abandoned or approached half-heartedly. Implementation has to be a formal step in the process, and all parties must appreciate that their work isn't done once the decision is made. You must be as disciplined in communicating out and driving implementation as you are in making the decision.

Consistent, transparent communication and follow-up requires answering the following questions:

- Who will be impacted or need to implement the decision? Who influences those who are impacted or will be called on to implement it?

- What do they need to know about the decision, why it was made and how it was made?

- What do they need to know or be able to do to implement it?

- What will be barriers to them implementing?

- How can you overcome these barriers through follow-up and communication with them?

Proactive management of the implementation that encourages ownership speeds up adoption of the implementation and can prevent the "fits and starts" that often characterize decision-making in matrix roles.

Following these five rules takes time but helps you pick up speed in the long term. Adjust your expectations and approach with this in mind. As a 25-year veteran of several large matrix organizations told me, "What I found, and I still find it, is that we view the process and the conversations that are part of getting matrix decisions made as a either a luxury or a speed bump. They are neither, and once we wrap our heads around this, we can get better at decisions and get better decisions." What will also help is our next Essential, Flex Your Influence Muscle. Whether you are trying to reach a decision or affect how people implement it, influence is required.

In decision-making in the matrix, you often need to go slow to go fast.

MINDSET

IN SUMMARY

EMBRACE

→ Inclusion balanced with speed is the name of the game in matrix decision-making

→ Good decisions require investments on the front-end in terms of thinking through the process and on the back-end to ensure implementation.

→ Gaining agreement is an investment, not only in the decision, but in the implementation of that decision.

→ Decision implementation in a matrix will take as much focused, concerted effort as the making of the decision.

TRY

→ Review your recent decisions. Were you broad enough in your input? Were you able to narrow who you included on making the decision?

→ To watch for bias, assign a watch dog on your team or a colleague (to watch you specifically). Ask this person to raise a flag when they see a bias playing into decision-making.

→ When you are making a decision as a team, keep the decision, the criteria and the bigger-picture goal visible—literally. If you are in a room together, have it on flipcharts. If working asynchronously, have it at the top of a page or beginning of a document that they are reviewing.

→ Review the implementation of your recent decisions. Are there certain people or parts of your matrix that you are neglecting in terms of communication and follow-up? What is that costing you?

IN PRACTICE

REPORTING RELATIONSHIP MATRIX

Decision-making is tricky here because you can often get caught in the middle of two bosses who have reached a stalemate on a decision that affects you, or you may be faced with making a decision that requires weighing their opinions or preferences. "Zoom Out" is what you will need to help them do or do yourself—take a look at the bigger-picture objective and determine the option that best gets you there. If you are helping them make a decision, you may have to do some of the set-up described in Rule #3 for them. Make sure they are both clear on the decision being made and even propose some criteria.

CUSTOMER HUB MATRIX

Customer input and implementation will be your two biggest challenges. You may be closer to the customer, so making sure your partners take the customer into account in their decision-making is key. Developing strong partnerships will mean inclusion in decision-making, which will provide you a window to make sure the customer voice is heard. In implementation of decisions you have made, make sure they understand the "why," especially from a customer's perspective. They may be removed from direct, frequent customer contact, so don't assume the "why" is obvious to them.

CROSS-FUNCTIONAL AND PROJECT TEAM MATRICES

Investing in agreement is critical here, as most of the decisions will be made as a team. Have a well laid-out, replicable process for making decisions and set parameters on how long you will strive for consensus and what happens when you can't reach consensus. Also, make very sure that the people on your teams are "deputized." Make sure they can make decisions for the functions they represent. If they are unable to make decisions and have to continually go back to their function for validation, you have the wrong person on the team or their functional boss/team is not clear on what their role is on your team.

ESSENTIAL #5

FLEX YOUR INFLUENCE MUSCLE

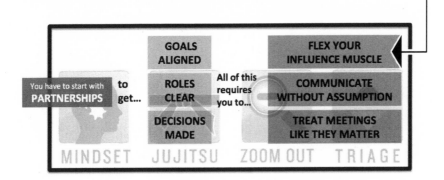

WHAT IT IS

In matrix roles, your accountabilities and responsibilities probably exceed your formal power. Lacking in power, influence is all you've got.

WHAT YOU WILL LEARN

» What builds influence muscle in matrix roles
» What to consider when deciding to wield your influence
» Seven key influence ingredients
» How to selectively elevate and delegate
» The power of patience and perseverance

RICH was a physician in a leadership role for a hospital system

change-out. With a solid line to the Chief Medical Officer and a dotted line to the Chief Information Officer, he was dead center at the intersection between the standardization aims of the IT department and the innovation ambitions of the clinicians at the hospital. This quote from my interview with him was striking:

> *"It's frustrating to go to work, engage in something I have a lot of passion and pride in and yet have so few victories."*

He went on to share a series of examples of his attempts to get traction and influence both sides of his matrix. IT expected him to drive standardization and get everyone on board. His fellow physicians expected him to influence IT so that they could "have it their way" in terms of system configuration. He said, "Every time I gain traction with the clinical side, IT says I am going rogue. Every time I gain traction on standardization, I am a hero in IT and the goat to physicians."

Added to this was the fact that the two sides also had very different expectations of the style and method of influence he would employ. His dotted line boss in IT told him, "Go out and kick their asses into line." His solid line boss on the clinical side implored him to "be nice and work with them."

Even the partnerships with the two bosses were polar opposites. His solid line was a long-time trusted colleague; his dotted line a new leader in the hospital with whom he had little history, and what history there was wasn't terribly pleasant. How did he influence?

> *"Small, short-term achievements that I set for myself keep me going—I see a lot that needs to be done but can't influence it all, so I stay focused. I also remind myself and anyone I come in contact with what the bigger picture is. It's not about what one side of the house or another thinks is right; it is about the path that we all eventually meet up with at the organizational level. And it's not about winning every battle with both sides of my matrix or pleasing both—that's impossible."*

His biggest mistake?

> *"Being too unwavering at the beginning. I wasn't willing to give or let them sway me. This only got them defensive and created barriers that I am breaking down now to influence them."*

BUILDING INFLUENCE MUSCLE IN MATRIX ROLES

Rich's concentration on influence is warranted. In conducting the research for this book, influence was second only to building relationships and trust as the most important matrix skill identified—all of which play off each other in the way you get things done. This is because crisscrossing lines of authority and accountability

leave matrix roles without much formal, sanctioned power. Fortunately, influence isn't something you have or you don't: it is a muscle you develop.

Stephen Covey begins *The Seven Habits of Highly Effective People* with the concept of Circle of Influence/Circle of Concern. Here's my interpretation of it and how it applies to influence in matrix roles.

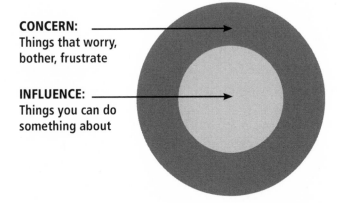

CONCERN:
Things that worry, bother, frustrate

INFLUENCE:
Things you can do something about

In Covey's description, among the concerns that enter your consciousness, there are some you can do something about and others you can't. His advice is to focus on those you can influence and let the others go—don't let them take up your time or energy. This is exactly what Rich does in setting his own "small short-term achievements." He stays focused on where he can influence.

Opportunities to influence abound in matrix roles—I realized this as I listened to Rich describe his situation. From his purview, he sees more than most people, which is not unique. Matrix roles are usually built around critical initiatives (in the case of project teams or cross-functional teams), critical intersections (in the case of dual-reporting relationships) or critical customers (in the case of a customer hub). Sitting at an intersection provides you with a unique vantage point—you see things that others haven't noticed yet. You see holes, issues, decisions that need to be made, conversations that need to take place. In Covey's terms, more enters your Circle of Concern.

All that extra matrix information entering your Circle of Concern can do funny things to your influence muscle in matrix roles. You can easily fall into one of two traps:

Under-utilized influence muscle =
VICTIM

Over-utilized influence muscle =
CONTROL FREAK

For some, the perspective and lack of formal power that are characteristic of matrix roles become overwhelming, and they go into victim mode, convincing themselves that they are powerless and blaming the matrix for everything. Others attempt to corral and control everything to gain comfort in the matrix, which is exhausting, dilutive and builds up resentment from the stakeholders around them. By overusing their influence they become like that billboard you see every morning on your way to work—at first it gets everyone's attention, but eventually it just blends in with the scenery.

DECIDING TO WIELD YOUR INFLUENCE MUSCLE

Rich, our subject from the opening story, was very judicious in wielding his influence. As a matter of fact, this is one of the things that kept him sane in his influence-rich role.

You should clearly act on issues that are within your sphere of influence and have a high impact on your team and/or project. By the same token, those issues that are not within your influence and have a low impact should be left by the wayside. But there are plenty of variations

> Those issues that are not within your influence and have a low impact should be left by the wayside.

TRIAGE

in between. Here is a way to think about triaging items that enter your Circle of Concern:

The idea here is that you have a range of options—from completely letting go to charging ahead at full throttle. Understanding this range helps you keep a balance. When you are triaging, be sure to challenge your historic boundaries. In a situation where your automatic assumption is that you can't influence, think again about what you could possibly do. If the issue is something that historically you have tackled but with mixed results, skip it and see how the situation plays out without your influence. Also, watch for items to shift either in impact or your influence level and readjust accordingly.

Jean-Luc is a director of Materials for a US-based manufacturing company. His story provides a good example of this type of balance. His daily triage of influence opportunities is driven by his solid line reporting relationship to his country manager in France and dotted line reporting relationship to the head of Global Supply Chain in the US. Here are three items that recently came across his desk:

OPPORTUNITY #1. The Global Supply Chain function has scheduled a week-long training session in the US in July (four months from now). The session conflicts with the vacation schedules of every member of his team.

> **Jean-Luc's Decision: Keep an eye on it.** These training times tend to shift, so he will give it one month and see if he then has to influence the timing.

OPPORTUNITY #2. The global project team he is on is designing an employee survey, and they want to distribute it in English only to save on expenses.

> **Jean-Luc's Decision: Tackle it.** This decision could completely derail the results for his location because there is no way they will get accurate responses to in-depth questions in a non-native language. He has a voice on the team and can call for backup if need be.

OPPORTUNITY #3. Jean-Luc's two bosses disagree over which vendor to choose for an important raw material.

> **Jean-Luc's Decision: Let it go.** There is not much he can do to influence either one of them on this issue. Realistically, the difference between the two vendors from his team's perspective is minimal.

Again, with so much coming at you that needs attention and influence, you have got to become good a distinguishing those that you need to invest time and energy and exert muscle on and those that have low return or little chance of traction.

INFLUENCE INGREDIENTS: PROACTIVE AND IN THE MOMENT

There are two types of people who can influence—those who are persuasive conversationalists and those who build up influence equity over time. Not surprisingly, the latter are the ones who can have sustained influence in the matrix.

In matrix positions you are either influencing a current partner (and through this influence opportunity have a chance to develop the partnership to the next level or leverage the current state of the partnership) or you are influencing someone who may well be a partner in the future. Influence in matrix roles rarely happens in isolation—it usually isn't the first or last interaction with the person you are trying to influence. What that means is that your level of influence starts well before you jot a few persuasive ideas down on paper or put together a couple of compelling PowerPoint slides. It also means that how you handle the opportunity to influence impacts not only the issue at hand but also your partnership and future influence prospects.

There are seven critical ingredients specific to influence in matrix roles that come into play. Three happen prior to influence; the other four, in the moment of influencing. Here's what they are and how they play out with the person you are trying to influence:

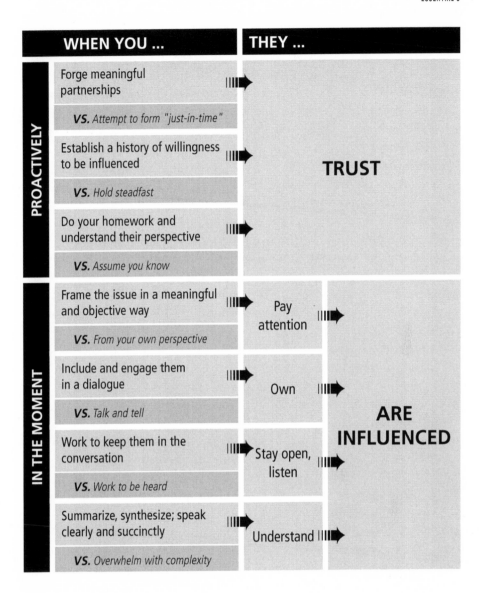

We will look at each of these ingredients individually, but know that for any given situation, you may not need all seven. Accomplish the three proactive ingredients well, and the in-the-moment ingredients don't have to be 100% buttoned-down. Chances are if these first three are in place, you are influencing Integrated or Collaborative Partners, which we know from Essential #1 goes a long way when you are attempting to influence.

But if you don't have the proactive ingredients in place, you will need to nail things in the moment. When trust is not established, you will have to fill the void with a highly effective dialogue.

THREE PROACTIVE INGREDIENTS

You reap what you sow when influencing in the matrix. The "sowing" includes forging partnerships in your matrix, building trust by demonstrating willingness to be influenced, and doing your homework to make sure you understand what you are attempting to influence from your partner's perspective.

PROACTIVELY FORGE MEANINGFUL PARTNERSHIPS. "Unequivocally, she cannot succeed here," an executive coach told one of my clients when asked if his new hire, Jeri, who had torn through an R&D group leaving the landscape barren, could be successful in the role. She had spent her first six months on the job bullying, threatening and strong-arming project teams to get things done. Her trust was shot, and people were now actively rallying against anything she wanted, just as a matter of principle. Instead of building partnerships, Jeri was building walls that were destroying any chance she had to build partnerships anywhere in the organization. Without partnerships, she couldn't influence.

A lot of heavy lifting is necessary to get things done in a matrix role, and partnerships lighten the load. When you have good partnerships, your influence grows, not just with the partners, but through them as well. Partners take you at face value and need far less convincing of your motives and the merit of your idea. Integrated and Collaborative Partners are high-trust partnerships. Where there is trust, there is influence. Where there isn't trust, you will need to make baseline investments and compound your investment, as outlined in Essential #1.

ESTABLISH A HISTORY OF WILLINGNESS TO BE INFLUENCED. Who has changed your mind at work? In the course I teach on leadership and change, we spend two weeks discussing interpersonal influence, and this is the first question I pose at the start of the module. Several times I have gotten the answer, "No one." Then, at least in my head, I direct my lectures and examples to that student. If I can open them up to influence, I will make them more influential.

Remember Rich's lesson learned in the opening story? He called himself "too unwavering." In order to influence, you must be willing—and demonstrate that willingness—to be influenced. This is especially true in matrix roles, where relationships are long term and inherently require much give-and-take. When you are steadfast and do more taking than giving in influence situations, trust can dwindle, making it difficult to influence.

DO YOUR HOMEWORK TO ENSURE YOU UNDERSTAND THEIR PERSPECTIVE. The target of your influence is most likely in a different function, division or location in the matrix than you. That means you cannot assume that you know the impact of what you are influencing on them, their operations and processes or team. The chances of creating unintended consequences are high. Look beyond your own area to understand the impact and reaction of those on the receiving end. It will prepare you for questions they will ask, concerns

Look beyond your own area to understand the impact and reaction of those on the receiving end of what you are trying to influence.

ZOOM OUT

or objections they will have and will tell them that you are thinking beyond your needs and self interests.

FOUR INGREDIENTS FOR INFLUENCE IN THE MOMENT

Next comes the conversation, when you introduce or frame the issue and work to have a constructive dialogue about what you want to accomplish and why. You will have to consider both the issue at hand and the relationship when you enter the conversation—you are aiming for wins on both sides. You may not always get wins, but going in with anything less in mind will undercut your approach.

FRAME THE ISSUE IN A MEANINGFUL AND OBJECTIVE WAY. The "frame" is the one-sentence statement you have in your mind in terms of what the issue is. There are many possible frames for any given issue. Do you frame it as a problem or an opportunity? As an investment or an expense? Do you frame the issue or the solution? A new product to consider or a chance to step into a new market?

Anne, a former colleague of mine, was once given the dubious task of "facilitating" her division's monthly senior leadership meetings with the General Manager (GM) and his 10 direct and dotted line reports (she reported to one of the team members). Everyone except the GM dreaded these meetings; he loved

> *"The greatest ability in business is to get along with others and to influence their actions."*
>
> JOHN HANCOCK

them. Everyone else described them as "talking heads giving updates on stuff that could have been emailed to me." No strategic talk, no problem solving, actually little interaction whatsoever. The team decided "it would be great" if Anne could "fix" the meetings.

She talked to each team member, summarized the feedback and talked to the GM about it. He nodded politely, said he'd think about it, thanked her for her time and stopped just shy of patting her on the head on the way out the door. So she tried a different tack. A week later, she sent him an email framing the situation in financial terms. She calculated the hourly salaries of each leader and then added in travel and other expenses. She changed her frame from "Your people think the time in these meetings could be better spent" to "Did you know you are spending $30,000 per month on these information sharing meetings? Is this your intended investment?" She heard back from him almost immediately. Reframing the problem got his attention. Once she had his attention, the influence was easy.

Jeffrey Pfeiffer, in *Managing with Power,* gives a lot of weight to how we frame an issue: "Establishing the framework within which issues will be viewed and decided is often tantamount to determining the result."

We often tend to frame things in one way—our own. Anne framed the meeting issue as she saw it—a problem with the level of engagement. That got her polite disregard. Framing from the recipient's point of view can get their attention right from the start.

Here are the keys to framing the issue or idea you are trying to influence:

Frame the issue in a way that is meaningful to your target. The first thing to do when you are establishing how you will frame the issue is to take the perspective of your target. Bill tells a great story of influencing people to make difficult personnel decisions:

> *"When I tried to influence new hiring managers to deal with problem performers, I came up against brick walls because they were afraid to hurt someone's feelings. It wasn't until I reframed it away from 'you need to get rid of this problem performer' to 'you need to do what is fair for the other team members that are picking up the slack' that they usually agreed to take action."*

Frame it in a larger context. You have to understand the bigger organizational context before you frame it. Business acumen is a key influence ingredient. Articulate how a change impacts the big picture outside your piece of the matrix. In the leadership-meeting example, Anne initially framed the leadership meetings in terms of what they meant to the participants, which was too narrow for the leader. When she positioned the meetings in the context of his division's investment decisions, she got his attention.

Frame it objectively. One of the leaders involved in this book told a wonderful story of a country manager from Italy. Each time he started down a path he wanted others to follow, he started with, "In my country…" He was given feedback letting him know that this influence tactic wasn't working. Framing it this narrowly, from only his perspective, immediately put others on the defensive and undermined the credibility of his view. Although he changed his wording, he still missed the point. He switched to, "In a country like mine…" To influence in a matrix, when possible, take it out of your personal context. This shows that you are influencing in the right direction and for the right reasons, and it makes your attempt more credible.

> Take it out of your personal context. This shows that you are influencing in the right direction and for the right reasons, and it makes your attempt more credible.
>
> **ZOOM OUT**

INCLUDE AND ENGAGE THEM IN A DIALOGUE. We have talked about the power of inclusion on adopting and implementing decisions—simply put, people adopt decisions quicker and integrate them more fully when they have been involved in them. The same is true of influence. People are more open to influence when you don't come to them with a *fait accompli*. That is not always possible; there are times when you need someone to do something very specific that has no gray around it. But when possible, walk in with some wiggle room and opportunity for them to put their fingerprints on it. Going in softer, with less defined needs, can work to your advantage in influencing (as well as likely improve your solution).

> Going in softer, with less defined needs, can work to your advantage in influencing (as well as likely improve your solution).
>
> **JUJITSU**

WORK TO KEEP THEM IN THE CONVERSATION. Attempts to influence often create conflict, and people don't have the courage or the appetite for conflict to stay in a conversation. They quit too soon. Keeping yourself and the other person in the dialogue is critical. One matrix leader I talked to called this the organizational equivalent of "never go to bed angry." Keep the conversation going until you both decide to shelve it. Pauses and walk-aways are good, but come back to the issue and make sure you both decide when the exchange is complete.

Let's go back to Anne's conversation with the General Manager about his atrocious meetings. Here are a few things Anne could do to help both of them stay in the conversation:

Keep the relationship front and center. Influence dialogues in matrix roles require the relationship to be front and center. Reminding yourself of this changes your tone and the words you choose. Reminding them elevates your dialogue to common ground.

> *"I am committed to being a valuable partner with you on this and the other initiatives we have ahead of us."*

Listen and acknowledge what they are saying. Once people sense that you aren't listening, you've lost them. They become defensive of their idea, determined to be heard instead of determined to work with you on the issue. People who are heard open themselves up to influence. Their questions are also valuable, in-the-moment data for you. What are they unclear about? What is holding them back from being influenced? What do they care about? This is exactly the type of information that you need to be influential, and you can't get it if you're talking all the time.

> *"I've heard you mention a couple of times the need you have to connect with people on a monthly basis; I think we can do that and meet some of the other needs they have."*

Restate the big picture and your common ground. When people start to sound defensive or agitated, take a step back and restate what the bigger objective is and what you have in common.

> *"There's no doubt we both want to make sure that the meetings are a strong investment in time and that they help you and the team drive the business."*

State what you are *not* saying. When people feel threatened they may take your comments to the extreme and begin to react to that extreme as opposed to your actual proposition.

> *"I am not suggesting that we scrap everything about the meetings."*

Reinforce your ability to reach agreement. Even when things get contentious, retain your optimism on reaching agreement and communicate that with the person you are talking to.

"I think between the two of us we can land on an approach to the meetings that meets your needs and the needs of your team."

BE CLEAR, SUCCINCT, SUMMARIZE AND SYNTHESIZE. Matrix roles and the organizations they reside in are complex, and those who simplify, succeed. Simplicity drives agreement. Reaching an agreement is dependent on your ability to simply and clearly state what is needed and why. If there are options to consider, they must be laid out clearly. Overwhelming already overwhelmed people with a complex description of a problem and its solution undercuts your efforts. If they are going to disagree, you want them to disagree on the merit of your proposal, not because they don't have the energy to figure out what you are requesting.

Simplifying might mean boiling things down into three key rationales or a handful of simple options. Visual support helps. Not 10 slides, but one table that outlines your cause and effect or options with their pros and cons.

These seven ingredients need to be applied with a genuine mindset of relationship building, long-term investment and inclusion—not just influence. Without this the ingredients become tactics and ring hollow. There is no guarantee of influence in any given situation, but approaching the situation with the right mindset and applying the ingredients set you up nicely for subsequent influence situations. In other words, you may lose a battle, but win the war.

> These seven ingredients need to be applied with a genuine mindset of relationship building, long-term investment and inclusion—not just influence.
>
> **MINDSET**

SELECTIVELY ELEVATING AND DELEGATING

Just because something enters your Circle of Concern and you decide to tackle it doesn't mean you must personally attempt to influence it. If you feel that the conversation may risk further damage to the partnership or simply believe that someone else would be more successful, pull him or her in. You might be able to use strong partners who view your proposal favorably as influencers over other stakeholders—"up" is not the only place to look when identifying an influence surrogate.

In Essentials #2 and #3 we talk about elevating goal and role issues. More general issues requiring influence can be elevated or delegated as well—but the same rules of how you approach and frequency apply.

Darryl, a VP of Marketing in the middle of a multi-country matrix positioned elevating to influence in this way:

> *"There is always a temptation to go over someone's head. Eventually you find someone who owns everyone. In my role, sometimes I am that guy where the matrix meets. I tell the people who work for me that at the beginning of the year, they have a six-shooter that has to last the entire year. If you want me to jump in and resolve a conflict or make a decision or influence someone, you have six shots, and you better sandbag because I guarantee you are going to need some at the end of the year when everyone is running to numbers."*

THE POWER OF PATIENCE AND PERSEVERANCE

Patience may be a virtue, but in a matrix role it is a necessity. You will go home most days feeling like you didn't accomplish anything in all of your attempts to mold and shape those in your matrix. But you did, and if you persist you will see progress. In the opening story for this chapter, Rich said, "It's frustrating to go to work, engage in something I have a lot of passion and pride in and yet have so few victories." I knew from talking to him that he had mastered the matrix more than he realized. But without patience and perseverance, he won't be able to see the progress that he is making.

> *"It would be difficult to exaggerate the degree to which we are influenced by those we influence."*
>
> ERIC HOFFER

I was pretty oblivious to the need for these traits well into my career in matrix roles. Then I had a boss, Mary, who changed everything. Mary was a bit of a Zen Master. Often I would find myself in influence mode and try to force things—convince the senior leadership team to invest in a project or induce my dotted line corporate boss to change a priority. I would run up against walls over and over again and land in Mary's office frustrated and bruised. "Susan, you are planting seeds," Mary would say, "If you measure your success in days and not months or even years, you are going to go crazy in this role."

Patience and perseverance are required to see the incremental progress you are making.

MINDSET

One of my upper management interviewees put patience into a great perspective:

> *"You have just got to do what is within your control to find the issue, shine a spotlight on it, frame it, present it. What someone else chooses to do with this information is truly above your pay grade—you can't control the big picture, only your role in it. Propose what needs to change, then pin it to somebody's chest, work through it with your boss, whoever. But just keep shining a spotlight on it."*

Get good at influencing in a matrix, and you can influence anywhere—it's like New York, if you can make it here, you'll make it anywhere. You are going to see so many things that need to change, improve or go away when you sit at an organizational intersection. Don't let the purview frustrate you—appreciate it and learn to pick and choose where you will make an impact. Your influence abilities, mixed with strong partnerships, underlie every skill, every success you will have in your role. When joined with our next essential, No Assumption Communication, you pack a powerful punch.

IN SUMMARY

EMBRACE

→ The long-term investment that is typical of influence in a matrix—history with people follows you into influence situations. The more positive the history, the higher the likelihood of success.

→ Being influenced, don't just focus on influencing. Your ability to do this increases your influence muscle.

→ The patience and perseverance that is required. Plant seeds and watch for incremental wins, not just the big wins.

TRY

→ When you are triaging, question your existing boundaries. Try to influence those things that you have previously let go because you didn't think you could impact it. If you have tackled an issue before with mixed results, let it go and see how the situation plays out without your influence.

→ Always think of at least one other frame for something you are influencing. Don't get anchored to the frame that comes to you first—chances are that it is your preferred frame, not your target's.

→ Learn from those who have been influential in your organization (not those with titles, those who got things done without a big title). Also enlist the help of people who have been able to influence the person you are trying to influence—leverage their knowledge and successes.

IN PRACTICE

REPORTING RELATIONSHIP MATRIX

When influencing two bosses, it can be easy to shoot for efficiency and apply the same approach to both of them. But they are two different people with different experience bases and roles that have been brought together by the matrix. They are coming from two different perspectives and will require different strategies. Also, although you can use one boss to influence the other when it makes sense, don't overuse this. It can easily create resentment and politics between the two.

CUSTOMER HUB MATRIX

The predominant influence situation you will find yourself in is influencing the priorities of the people in your hub—trying to get your priority to be their priority. Influence through motivating is key here. This type of matrix and influence requires a partnership that is at least at a strong transactional level. Follow the Help-Me-Help-You Rules in Essential #1 to establish the necessary trust. Then make sure you are connecting them to the customer needs (they are likely removed from this) and finally influence by motivating them on their contribution to the bigger-picture success.

CROSS-FUNCTIONAL AND PROJECT TEAM MATRICES

Your influence will likely be around accountability in this type of matrix role. Essential #7 will cover meetings—these will be your prime influence vehicles. You will likely be influencing a team of people, and meetings can provide motivation and a forum for accountability. Also, when your team needs to influence someone outside the team, leverage team members. Not all influence needs must be met by you.

ESSENTIAL #6

COMMUNICATE WITHOUT ASSUMPTIONS

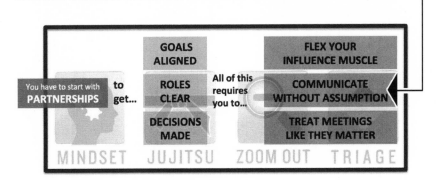

WHAT IT IS

Communicating in a matrix role is challenging—a constant stream of information needs to be absorbed, analyzed and shared with others in your matrix. To pick up speed we make assumptions on who needs to know what, how they prefer to hear it and even what we ourselves need to know. These assumptions can lead to communication misfires that impact not only your work product but also your trust and credibility.

WHAT YOU WILL LEARN

» Assumptions and what they lead to
» Under-communicating: risks and remedies
» Over-communicating: risks and remedies
» Casting a wide net: communicating to the right people
» Yours is not theirs: communicating in the right way
» Assumption-free listening

PATRICK leads a six-person new product development project. He is in a meeting with his boss and

several others from across the matrix, including Annette, one of his team member's bosses. In the meeting it is announced that they will be adding one more level of testing for his project, which will push the deadline back six months. Coming out of the meeting, he passes by two project team members and lets them know. That afternoon he is in a meeting with two other project team members and lets both of them know. That leaves Mark, the sixth member of the team. Mark reports to Annette, who was in the meeting. Patrick figures that connection will ensure Mark is informed, so he doesn't need to reach out. A few days later, the team convenes and starts working out a new plan, with the new deadline. Mark is confused, in the dark and frustrated to be caught unprepared. This isn't the first time he has been caught flat-footed with this team. He makes up all kinds of stories about why Patrick told everyone but him—none of which is as innocuous as the simple assumption Patrick made. Eventually all Mark's assumptions start to show up in how he communicates with the team—how much he shares, how engaged he is. The team reacts by retracting as well.

Patrick fell into a trap that is common to matrix roles. To streamline a messy matrix he made all kinds of assumptions and got himself in all kinds of trouble. Drawn out, this assumption cycle looks something like this:

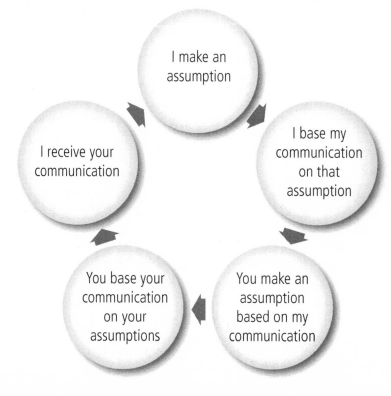

Caught in this vortex, our communication becomes based more on assumption than fact, and things can go downhill fast. This cycle can happen in any context, but even more so in matrix roles because of the sheer number of people we interact with and messages we are bombarded with. Mixed, incomplete and garbled messages are inevitable. Several leaders I talked to compared communication in a matrix to the game "Telephone," where the message starts out crystal clear to the initiator, is passed along from person to person and ends in a jumbled mess.

Consider this visual comparison of communication in traditional roles versus in a matrix role:

TRADITIONAL ROLE   MATRIX ROLE

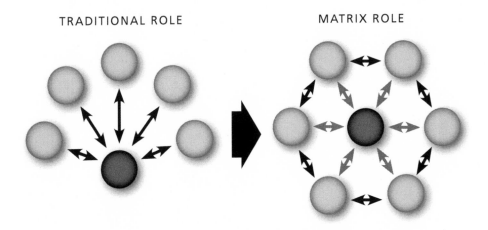

In a matrix not only do you have more people to communicate with (more circles, as shown above), you also have some interest in and even responsibility for the communication that takes place *between* the people in your matrix (just like Patrick in the opening story). This multi-directional, once-removed communication makes things especially challenging.

All these extra circles and arrows lead us to look for shortcuts, and that's where assumptions come in. Assumptions are everywhere. If we acted without them, we would never get anything done—we would always be waiting for the full picture to appear before taking a step. But often, the time these assumptions save upfront is negated by time spent later making amends and resolving miscommunications. These shortcuts catch up with you.

Often you won't even realize that you are operating on an assumption until someone does or says something in direct conflict with that assumption. About three conversations into my relationship with my book designer, he provided printing price quotes and gave me examples of a lot of terrific booklets under 100 pages. In the tote sitting next to me, I had brought examples of 200-page hardcover business books I admired. How did we get that far into a project with such divergent assumptions? My assumption was so ingrained that I didn't even know I had it—I didn't even think of telling him!

I am going to make a big, sweeping counter-intuitive statement about communication in matrix roles: *assumptions, not skills, are the biggest barriers to effective communication.* As a more intuitive follow-up declaration: *trust is predicated on communication.* Challenge your assumptions, improve your communication and grow your trust. If you don't cultivate trust, matrix roles simply do not work, or they collapse under the weight of all the processes and policies needed to make them work, as we learned in Essential #1.

ASSUMPTIONS AND WHAT THEY LEAD TO

So, here's how it goes. You are moving fast and you assume:

- » They know.
- » They don't know.
- » Somebody else already told them.
- » They don't need to know.
- » I'm the one to tell them.
- » I know how to tell them (or it doesn't matter how I tell them).
- » I know the whole picture.

These assumptions—and all their variations—cause us to make a number of blunders in matrix roles. We often find ourselves:

- » Under-communicating
- » Over-communicating
- » Communicating to the wrong people
- » Communicating in the wrong way
- » Not listening

And the result is:

- » Perceptions of information hoarding, politicking and other suspicions
- » Confusion
- » Lack of information or misinformation

These outcomes all lead to lack of trust, which means slower decision-making, decreased decision quality and less influence for you.

Let's take a look at the risks and remedies for each of these missteps.

UNDER-COMMUNICATING

Rebecca was an academic researcher who transferred to a corporate role advising pharmaceutical research. She went from one of the most independent roles out there to a matrix, dependent on and connected to many, many others. Communication was her nemesis. She continually under-communicated because she thought people knew, didn't need to know or that the reasons behind her actions and decisions were inherently obvious. The researchers and academics she was surrounded by in her previous life had low information needs beyond what was in front of them—she was the expert and they followed her lead. Now she was surrounded by people who needed to know what was going on inside her head, and she wasn't sharing it readily, if at all.

Rebecca quickly found out that in matrix roles, people have higher information needs—period. Overlapping roles and goals, ambiguity and close collaboration all increase the appetite for information. Those in your matrix will need to know more than your peers in a traditional organization might.

Rebecca's failure to broadcast brought on many unintended consequences that are prevalent among under-communicators:

- People around her filling in the blanks themselves (and acting upon them)
- Rebecca or others making decisions downstream without all the information
- People finding information out from others and feeling duped
- Others caught flat-footed when they are approached with the information

There are four things to keep in mind in terms of the communication needs of others: (1) they don't know what you know; (2) you don't necessarily know what they need to know; (3) the reason behind your actions is important to people and not inherently obvious and (4) when asked for information, your response matters.

THEY DON'T KNOW WHAT YOU KNOW. Whether it is expertise acquired over time or information acquired day-to-day, it's tough to appreciate what you know that others don't. Brian, a consultant to matrix organizations, put it best:

> *"There are few things harder than knowing what it's like to <u>not</u> know what you know. And therefore, you assume that other people must know it."*

This is made tougher by the fact that we often assume someone else is communicating to the people in our matrix—just like the story of Patrick and Mark. Remember the extra arrows that represented communication between the people in your matrix? They often fall apart. Both your solid line boss and your dotted line boss attend the same weekly leadership team meeting. That means they talk, right? So if you tell one, that message gets through to the other, right? Wrong. You are in a meeting with the manager of one of the people in your "hub." Important information on an upcoming customer visit is shared. Your hub member's boss will tell her, right? Probably not—that boss is probably making the same assumption about you!

Regardless of what drives your assumption of someone else's knowledge, you have to flip the switch and go from assuming they know to assuming they don't. Here's a great analogy. My oldest daughter plays fast-pitch softball. During her first year of true competitive play, the pitchers were much better and much faster than she was accustomed to. She was in a serious batting slump, and assumptions were partially to blame. She was used to pitchers who rarely threw strikes—so at the plate she assumed that the pitch coming at her was a ball and would only talk herself into swinging if it happened to be a strike. But these girls threw more accurately and faster, which meant that her assumption didn't work—pitches were flying right past her and into the catcher's glove before she could decide to swing. She had to switch her assumption from "it will be a ball" to "it will be a strike" in order to make contact with the ball. In other words, changing her assumption made her much more successful.

You have to shift from assuming they know to assuming they *don't*, and communicate accordingly.

MINDSET

This mental shift is the same one we have to make in a matrix—from assuming they know to assuming they don't, and that *not* communicating (like watching a pitch go by) is the exception rather than the rule. This means that with every bit of information coming toward you, your first question should always be, "Who needs to know?"

As information comes in, always ask yourself "Who needs to know?"

TRIAGE

YOU DON'T NECESSARILY KNOW WHAT THEY NEED TO KNOW. Sometimes we under-communicate because we don't think another person needs to know. Rebecca truly couldn't understand why in the world anyone would care about her work. After all—it was *her* work.

What makes us think that we are experts in the information needs of others? Remember the last time you walked out of your boss's office with marching orders, only to find out that what you just committed to doing by the end of the day required more information than you had at your finger tips? If you don't always have a firm grasp on your *own* information needs, why would you assume you have it for someone else's?

IF...	THEN...
You are in a meeting	In the margins note what you will need to communicate, to whom and how after the meeting
You get an email with information	Think "forward" not just "reply"
You have multiple stakeholders that connect	Don't assume they talk, leave nothing to chance (better they hear it twice than not at all)
You are in doubt as to their need to know	When in doubt, shout it out

Don't guess at another person's information needs—ask them. Information needs are not immediately obvious in a matrix. When you can, plan. Set up a process with your partner that ensures you are sharing pertinent information in the most effective and efficient way. There are going to be far more people to get messages out to, so you have got to become efficient at this. Establish a quick way to identify who needs to know and get out the information. Making this practice part of your continual, in-the-moment thought process and executing it with discipline will make you more effective and efficient. Dean, a finance manager on six different projects, had a cheat sheet and corresponding email distribution list for each of the projects he was on: "I just made it automatic, so it was easy to get out and just part of my process."

YOUR "WHY" IS NOT OBVIOUS. We assume that people inherently know and appreciate the reason behind our actions and decisions. Why is he here for a visit? Why is she asking these questions about the project plan? Why did he decide to bring in a consultant? Why did she push back the deadline?

Why, indeed. Our actions make perfect sense to us (or at least they should!). Inside our heads, the steps we took and our full rationale is laid out. The problem is that no one else can see inside our heads. In a matrix role this becomes increasingly dangerous, because of the number of people who are involved and the corresponding stories they can make up and propagate about the rationale behind your actions.

If remembering to communicate the "what" of your knowledge is challenging (as per the previous section), then the "why" doubles down on that challenge. We assume the "why" is inherently obvious, but it rarely is. People are smart, and the "what" alone isn't enough for them. They need to know the "why." If they don't, they will fill in the blanks.

We tend to attribute our decisions and actions to positive intent. But as for the decisions and actions of others, we lean more toward assuming the worst. David Grossman, Founder and CEO of the communication consultancy The Grossman Group, says it best:

> *"Given two ways to interpret what's behind an action or decision, people inevitably choose the most harmful of the choices."*

So be as readily transparent and forthright with the "why" behind your actions as you are with the "what." Don't make them guess—believe me, you won't like their guess!

How can we stop ourselves from making the assumption that they know our intentions? Here are a few options:

- Provide the complete picture and context. Use the journalist's rule of covering the who, what, why and when.

- Don't wait for them to ask why—give the information upfront.

- When asked "why," assume they are curious, not questioning, and answer in a way that encourages future "why" questions and discourages filling in the blanks.

WHEN PEOPLE ASK, YOUR RESPONSE MATTERS. Maureen, a supply chain manager, told me about a person who worked for her. His biggest failing in his matrix role? Taking questions too personally. He took every question as a personal affront to his skills, experience and effectiveness. Ultimately, it cost him his job.

The increased information appetite in matrix organizations means more questions. Take them for what they are—don't personalize, don't take offense, don't assume they are trying to disprove your expertise. Answer questions with patience and sincerity—regardless of how others respond in return. In a matrix, you accomplish things with and through other people: that requires dialogue. And that dialogue includes questions. If you take questions personally, you won't get very far, because your defensiveness will show and affect the level of trust that people have in you.

Answer questions with patience and sincerity—regardless of how others respond in return.

JUJITSU

Joellen, a government affairs manager, thought of questions as a positive challenge. She put it this way:

"I see it as my personal challenge to make sure they are in the know. Whenever they have to ask for an update, I ask myself, 'OK, where did I blow it? What was I assuming?' My goal is to never have them ask for something I should have given them automatically."

OVER-COMMUNICATING

Richard was a new director of IT who moved from a small privately held company to a large corporation. I was brought in to coach him on his transition—which was not going well at all. I spoke to about 10 people he worked with—employees, partners, bosses. One theme came out loud and clear. He wasn't communicating enough—everyone felt in the dark. I gave him the feedback, and we discussed ideas on how to improve. Six weeks later, I circled back to the people I talked to. Their new complaint? He was flooding them with emails and updates, and they were drowning in information.

Richard's lesson was that simply swinging the pendulum from under-communicating to sharing every tidbit of information you get with your entire email distribution list is not really the answer. In today's world of information overload, you can't just add to the avalanche of information. People feel over-communicated with when you provide a lot of information that:

» Is perceived as irrelevant to their needs
» Isn't user friendly to get through
» Appears self-serving in nature

Some people think the key to successful matrix communication is the "Cc" field and the "Forward" button on their computer. But simply forwarding information on is often not enough. Here are a few steps you should take to ensure that you are hitting the right balance in your communication:

FROM THE GET GO	Ask: What information can I share on an ongoing basis that would be helpful?
	Ask: What is the best way to provide it?
IN THE MESSAGE	Tell: Here's why I am sharing this with you.
	Tell: Here's the information that is most important.
	Ask: Was this information helpful? Is this the kind of information I should continue to send your way?
	Cc: Only those who really need to know, and let people know why they are Cc'd.
ONGOING	Ask: Are you are getting what you need from me? What information is most helpful? Least?

Over-communication happens in live form as well—but often less so, because we can self-correct in real time. Watch for cues such as eye contact, nodding and questions or statements that directly relate to what you are saying. Over the phone, focus on the verbal cues such as relevant questions and statements. An absence of these cues might mean that you have communicated completely but excessively or that they don't perceive the information as important enough to listen to and form questions or comments around.

Both in person and over the phone, be very, very conscious of the balance of dialogue. If it's not 50/50, pull back. Let them ask questions to guide the discussion—don't think you have to answer everything before they have a chance to ask a question. Monologues (another form of over-communicating) don't come close to the productivity of dialogues.

Over-communicating is still less risky for trust building than information hoarding in a matrix role. Richard's incessant forwarding and updating annoyed people, but they didn't doubt his motives. On the other hand, in Rebecca's case, her under-communication led to speculation and stories, creating a dynamic that took months to mend. Let them tell you (or even better, outright ask them) if the information is unnecessary. But don't assume.

> Let them ask questions to guide the discussion—don't think you have to answer everything before they have a chance to ask a question.
>
> JUJITSU

CAST A WIDE NET: COMMUNICATING WITH THE RIGHT PEOPLE

Two realities in matrix roles should challenge your assumptions about "who needs to know." The first we have already talked about—information appetites are higher in matrix roles. Not only do people need to know more, but more people need to know. The second is that to some extent the matrix neutralizes titles and levels. Who you interact with doesn't always line up with your title. I talked to people who led projects with team members one or two titles up, even a few who led teams on which their own boss was a team member. You may partner on equal ground with someone two steps below and in another function.

You will also find yourself a target of communication from many different directions. All bets are off in matrix organizations regarding the hierarchy of who talks to whom. Get used to it, and don't let the organizational chart be your guide to whom to communicate to and whom to receive communication from.

These realities mean you will have to cast a wider net in your communication. More people will need to know and you will be the one expected to tell them—regardless of your level or theirs.

Phillip, an engineer and project manager, put it this way, "I just figure out how many people I think need to know and then double that—it gets me in the ballpark." He was being facetious, but you do need to push yourself on who needs to know and realize that there are probably more than you think.

> You will always have to cast a wider net in your communication than you initially assume.
>
> ZOOM OUT

Not only do matrix roles require a wider net of communication, they also challenge the traditional assumption that your boss is your most important audience. He or she is not. As a matter of fact, your boss may need to know significantly less and at a significantly lower level of detail than others in your matrix. More than likely, the real work gets done through communicating everywhere but up. Of course your boss shouldn't be in the dark, but he/she is not your only audience or at times your most important audience. When I review multi-source (360) feedback with matrix leaders, it is almost always the peers and subordinates who feel the most in the dark. The motivation to communicate with your boss may be clear, while the motivation to communicate with those around you may be less so. But placing too great an emphasis on communicating up is a mistake—not only will others in your matrix be less informed than they need to be, but they will also make assumptions about the reasons behind your focus on upward communication.

To ensure that you are both balanced and complete in your communication to your matrix, make sure you think about the following:

- Know who does what so you know where to direct communication.

- Use visual cues to help you remember whom you need to get certain messages to (project team lists, email lists, etc.).

- Push yourself to think of one more person when you think your list is complete.

- When in doubt, shout it out.

- Beware of the "out of sight/out of mind" communication trap—take extra steps to communicate to those who are not co-located with you.

YOURS IS NOT THEIRS: COMMUNICATING IN THE RIGHT WAY

Figuring out how to communicate is where the diversity of the people in the matrix really becomes obvious. The more you interact outside of your immediate functional area, the fewer assumptions you can make about a person's communication preferences and level of understanding. In your corner of the world, people may share preferences and levels of expertise—to the point that you may appear to be "talking in code" to others. When venturing outside your corner, those assumptions can get you in trouble.

UNDERSTAND THEIR PREFERENCES. We tend to give what we want to get in communication. If we prefer email, we email everyone; if we like face-to-face, we assume everyone does; if we like to jump right into details, then that's how we deliver information to others.

Here's a great example of assuming your communication preference is theirs:

> Mary to Susan: *Those long voicemail summaries you leave me at the end of the day drive me absolutely crazy—can you just drop me voicemails on single issues?*

> Susan to Edward: *Those top-of-mind emails you leave me throughout the day drive me nuts—can you just leave me a summary at the end of the day?*

Yes, those were actual conversations from my boss to me and then from me to one of my employees. In both cases, Edward and I were assuming that our individual communication preferences (for me, it was a "daily digest" and for him it was single-topic messages) were also the preferences of our bosses.

There are as many communication preferences as there are people to have them. The point is not to create custom messages around every person in your matrix. But when the stakes are high or when you are working with someone on an ongoing basis, preferences matter. Get to know the preferences of the key people in your matrix—what do they need to know and how do they want to receive it. Don't assume they like to hear it the same way you do. This helps ensure your message doesn't misfire because of the way it was delivered.

With partners you will work with on an ongoing basis, get some of these preferences out on the table. A few questions to ask:

- What kinds of information do you prefer via email, voicemail or in person?

- Where's the best starting point for a discussion? Are you a "Give me the bottom-line, and I will ask questions" type, or do you prefer I start at the beginning with all the details?

- When's the best time to catch you live? Do you mind drop-bys, or would you rather I set up time formally?

UNDERSTAND WHAT THEY UNDERSTAND. Another trap we fall into is having our expertise cloud how we deliver a message. In sharing that expertise we can sometimes assume they know—and talk way over their heads—or assume they don't know and condescend to the point of distraction.

The matrix brings a variety of expertise together to reach a common goal. But all that expertise can be underutilized if everyone talks like they would back in their home base. Being able to translate technical expertise—be it financial, scientific, operational, etc.—is becoming as important as having the expertise in the first place. Not only using language that is jargon-free but stopping to define jargon that is especially critical to understanding is a daily requirement in a matrix role. Contextualizing technical information through examples and stories is also important. To communicate technical information effectively in your matrix you must not only be clear but connect the information to your audience.

> "If you talk to a man in a language he understands, that goes to his head. If you talk to him in his language, that goes to his heart."
>
> NELSON MANDELA

What you don't need to do is preface all your technical explanations. Helen, a physician, was partnering with Tom, an IT leader, on the implementation of a new electronic process for a hospital network. Tom had a habit of starting conversations off with "You probably don't realize it, but…" As a well-educated, highly successful surgeon, Helen didn't take too kindly to this—especially after she began a master's degree in an IT-related field. As she tells the story, "I couldn't wait for an opportunity to pounce on his comment and tell him how much I really did understand and realize all that he was talking about." Tom's assumptions got in the way of Helen trusting him and working with him—she started to shut him out.

It's hard to strike a balance between sharing in layman's terms and not coming off as condescending. It's also hard to appreciate and translate your expertise or to stop yourself from jumping in when you know you have the technical expertise and they don't. You are going to be faced with this a lot in a matrix—again, that is the point of a matrix, bringing together a diversity of expertise.

In either case—assuming they know or don't know, here are a few ways to keep your expertise in check:

RULE OF THUMB	WHAT IT SOUNDS LIKE
Provide expertise without arrogance or impatience.	"Stop me if this is redundant or if I am telling you something you already know," "What else can I answer?"
Ask if they are interested in learning more.	"Is this helpful? Should I keep going?"
Find out what they know by asking questions (in a non-threatening way).	"What would be most helpful for you to know? I don't want to bore you with details that aren't important."
Provide information in layman's terms and check to see if you slipped in any jargon.	"I'm close to this, so it is second nature to me—Did I explain that clearly? Any technical terms that I breezed by?"

ASSUMPTION-FREE LISTENING

Our focus so far has been on how we communicate out. But assumptions can also affect the way we take in information. Think about how you listen when the topic is one you know well versus one that is new. Right now you may be skimming this chapter because you feel saturated with "how-tos" on communication—what could this chapter offer that is new and different? When we assume we have the full picture, we stop really listening (or in this case reading)—when we aren't curious, our brains move on to other topics.

In a matrix role, listening is the bridge between your expertise and those of the people in your matrix. Without listening to each other, you are just two experts on parallel paths who may never meet to create what is intended.

However, this doesn't mean you have to listen with the intent of understanding everything around you. I distinctly remember the meetings I sat through in my first foray into a matrix role. I was very used to projects and corresponding meetings that fell directly into my area of expertise. All of the sudden I was in meetings where I didn't understand 95% of what they were talking about. I would take copious notes on all the terms, acronyms and concepts that I didn't know and bring them back to my boss for answers. She would patiently answer what she could. After several of these Q&A sessions, she said to me, "Susan, you aren't expected to know all of this—that's not your role. The point is not for you to be as expert as them, it is to pull out what you need to do your job."

> You don't have to listen with the intent of understanding everything around you; learn to let some information go.
>
> TRIAGE

To her credit, telling me that (as well as being unafraid to demonstrate that she didn't know all of it either) helped me put what I needed to understand in perspective.

Assumption-free listening is about realizing you don't have the full picture, asking genuine questions when you need to and actually absorbing the answers you receive. Janet, a customer service leader, learned this lesson the hard way after coming into a new matrix and "assuming that they hadn't thought of any of this and that's why they brought me in." After more than a few missteps and a few months of repair work, her mantra became, "Appreciate what happened before you got here."

I would add that it is not only "what happened before you got here" but also "what happens when you're not here." Whether it is a new project or a new person or team you are working with, you only have a small slice of the information on their history, role and responsibilities. Don't assume it is anything more than a small slice. A little listening with curiosity and humility goes a long way toward not only gathering useful information for your problem solving and decision-making, but also in building the partnership.

Assumptions stop us from hearing anything that doesn't match up with what we hold in our heads, and they stop us from being curious and asking questions. When you walk in without assumptions, you're automatically going to be a better questioner and listener. For assumption-free listening, keep these things in mind:

Ask two more questions. Even when you think you know the person, find two questions to ask them about themselves. When you think you know all the nuances of the problem, ask two more questions. Think you get all the ramifications of the solution? Ask two more questions.

Ask questions like a 3-year old. Why, Why, Why. Any parent of a young child will tell you that the "Why" stage is both exciting (because it shows their intellectual growth) and frustrating (because it can be all-consuming, and you don't have the all the answers). Asked with genuine curiosity, the question of "Why" is a great assumption breaker, especially when you think you already know the answer. Just make sure you ask the "why" without the "whine."

Don't match their defense with more defense. People are not used to being asked questions—they are used to people assuming and doing. So when you start asking questions, you

> Keep your tone non-defensive and express your (genuine) appreciation for taking time to answer your questions. **JUJITSU**

may get a little defense from them in return. That's ok; the only thing you can do is to keep your tone non-defensive and express your (genuine) appreciation for taking time to answer your questions.

Absorb it. All of this inquisitiveness doesn't do much good if you don't absorb and apply the information you acquire. The first step to absorbing it is simply restating it. Restating helps you mentally register the information (far more than just hearing it) and tells the other person that you heard them. As a further step, add a "so that's why" at the end to connect the dots between their answer and your experience. For example, if you ask a person in your hub how requests are prioritized, respond to their answer by adding: "OK, so that's why when I ask for customer return data I hear back pretty quickly, but the lead time on contract changes is longer."

Matrix roles are built around complex projects with lots of history and complex problems with many tentacles. You partner with people who have different experiences and styles. Nothing is straightforward, including your communication. Be prepared for this—realizing the challenges can help you turn off your assumptions. Once your assumptions are disabled, your communication and listening skills can fully develop and ultimately drive your results. And you will need all of those communication and listening faculties as you enter the realm of matrix meetings, which is the focus of Essential #7.

IN SUMMARY

EMBRACE

→ The higher-than-usual information needs of people in the matrix

→ People asking you a lot of questions about your work

→ The risk of over-communicating

→ The communication styles and preferences of your partners

→ What you don't know—be an assumption-free listener

TRY

→ When you get information, the first thing you should ask is, who needs to know this?

→ When you participate in a meeting, note everything that you will need to share with someone after the meeting in the margins or italics. Then you can easily skim your notes and identify what to communicate and to whom.

→ Challenge yourself to stay one step ahead of people on updates. If your boss beats you to the punch and asks you for an update, figure out why—did you think they knew? Didn't need to know? File that away for next time.

→ Even when you think you know a person, find two questions to ask them about themselves. When you think you know all the nuances of the problem, ask two more questions. Think you get all the ramifications of the solution? Ask two more questions.

→ Set up a rhythm for your communication. People trust communication that comes out consistently in terms of content, timing and format. They trust that they are getting the full story and become really good at grabbing the information they need.

IN PRACTICE

REPORTING RELATIONSHIP MATRIX

Your two bosses may have vastly different communication needs and preferences. There will be some you should cater to, some that you can't. The key here is not to assume that the communication preferences of one boss are shared by the other. When you are consciously choosing not to cater to a preference, be transparent about it: "Judy, I know you prefer we talk about this in person. But Jack has requested I document it, so I am providing the basics to you both in writing. Let me know if that poses a problem."

Also be very conscious about geographic differences. Chances are that one of your bosses is co-located with you and the other is not. Don't let the convenience of the onsite boss dictate your communication approach. It's easy to do, so avoid it by setting up ongoing, specific times to catch up with your remote boss.

CUSTOMER HUB MATRIX

This is probably the most challenging type of matrix role when it comes to communicating. You have multiple partners all in different functions, perhaps even different locations, and unlike the Cross-functional and Project Team Matrix Roles you probably don't have regular meetings that include everyone in your hub. Be very deliberate about how you communicate. Set up a process and rhythm for your communication—reliable timing, consistent content and formatting, etc. People trust communication that comes out consistently. If they trust that they are getting the full story, they will become really good at grabbing the information they need.

CROSS-FUNCTIONAL AND PROJECT TEAM MATRICES

Your key challenge in this type of role is translation. You will have to make sure that critical technical information is shared and absorbed effectively. If you are leading the team, take frequent pauses to allow questions or even better pose the questions yourself. This shows team members that it is OK not to understand all of the information on the first pass. If you are a team member, don't be afraid to ask the question—don't assume you are the only one with that question, because chances are you are not.

ESSENTIAL #7
MAKE MEETINGS MATTER

WHAT IT IS
Like relationships, meetings are not separate from results—they are *how* results are achieved in matrix roles. Get really good at meetings, and you will have better partnerships and be more influential. The results will follow.

WHAT YOU WILL LEARN
» The right mindset for approaching meetings
» Six steps to meetings that people want to be a part of
» What to do when you aren't leading the meeting

YOU will be tempted to skip this chapter. You have heard it all before—you know what it takes to run a meeting. Or maybe you think you are too junior or too senior to worry about this skill. WAKE UP! In a matrix role, regardless of your level, meetings are absolutely, positively critical—this is where the pieces of the matrix actually come together. You have to get them right or your matrix will splinter. Read on…

I distinctly remember the first matrix project team meeting I ever attended. Prior to walking into the meeting my boss told me, "Wait 'til you meet Pete, the project lead, he leads the best meeting I have ever been in."

I brushed the remark off, determined not to be impressed, for I, too, was known to lead a pretty decent meeting.

But what I saw in that conference room that day blew me away. Here was this guy, laid back, unassuming—I didn't even know he was the project lead until he kicked off the meeting—who led a meeting like I had never seen before. He was a master. It was like my career to date had been comprised of black and white, and I was just introduced to high-definition technicolor.

He laid out the plan for the meeting, he called people out, he connected dots, he challenged, he pulled us back from tangents, pulled us out of the forest so that we could see the trees. At the end he was able to present back a neat summary of where we had been, what we decided and who was on the hook for what for the next meeting. He was able to take all this raw material that we brought in and turn it into a real work product.

I walked out of the meeting completely pumped to be part of the project. I felt like we could take on the world, heck I felt like I personally could take on the world. He took this behemoth of a project stretching multiple oceans and functional lines and simplified it, made it doable.

Until you have been in a meeting like that, you don't see the potential for power. Motivation and influence are two key requirements in matrix roles, and meetings can be your tool. In a matrix role, meetings are the forum for avoiding and resolving collisions and producing results by bringing together divergent goals, opinions and experiences.

The meetings that are convened in matrix roles are definitely not run-of-the-mill meetings—there is so much at stake. They are the most visible, public display of your abilities as a matrix manager. They give you the potential to motivate through inclusion and build ownership where you can't motivate through incentives or authority. We spend time and invest dollars trying to reward, recognize and ultimately motivate people. What motivates people? Getting stuff done. Friends, peers and camaraderie also motivate people. Do you know where you get stuff done while simultaneously surrounding yourself with friends, peers and comrades? Meetings! Meetings have great potential. But that potential is seldom realized.

As discussed in Essential #5, your formal power is limited in a matrix role, but the need to influence is seemingly unlimited. Do you know where you can build influence? You guessed it: a meeting. Show people you are disciplined and can drive to a result while respecting their time, and you become an influencer.

IT STARTS WITH THE RIGHT MINDSET

The title of this Essential really says it all concerning the mindset that is absolutely necessary—*meetings matter.* Valuing meetings as the powerful, productive, motivating force that they really can and should be should come before any agenda or meeting management tactic you employ. Placing a value on meetings transforms them from an interruption to a critical function and opportunity.

Meetings matter; give them the treatment they deserve.

MINDSET

With this assumption in mind, the time you put in upfront shifts—you put more in and voila! You get more out.

MEETINGS ARE NOT A DEPARTURE FROM WORK, THEY ARE YOUR WORK. "I was in meetings all day, I didn't get anything done." How often have you heard or said that? The first thing we need to do is shift that way of thinking. Meetings that are called for the right reason and managed in the right way (both of which we will talk about later) are not an intrusion on your productivity; they are the vehicle for your productivity. This is especially true in a matrix role—meetings are the way different sides of the matrix come together. Without them the matrix fragments.

Meetings have become a caricature of themselves. It is much more entertaining to complain about a really bad meeting than rave about one that was super-productive. But if we stop thinking about meetings as if they are vast conspiracies to hijack precious work time, the rest of the mindsets and skills will fall into place.

YOU GET OUT OF MEETINGS WHAT YOU PUT INTO THEM. Jeanine is pulling 10 people together to talk about data she collected on a customer visit. She is stretched to the max and doesn't have an hour prior to the meeting to plan it, but she figures everybody has the general gist of what needs to happen. She walks into the meeting and spends the first 20 minutes going over why everyone is here and what they are going to discuss. They get into the conversation and the hour is up. So she schedules another meeting to finish things up. She walks into meeting #2 and starts by refreshing everyone's memory about what they covered last time, why she wanted to talk about it in the first place and where the conversation left off. This catch-up eats up 30 minutes. They get into the meat of the topic and then the meeting is over. So what does she do? Jeanine decides that next time they need to meet for two hours instead of one!

Jeanine is getting out of these meetings exactly what she is putting in: nothing. A one-hour meeting is turning into a four-hour meeting with no end in sight. Too bad she didn't have that one hour upfront to think it through.

If meetings really matter, put in the time beforehand to really think them through—desired outcomes and structured agenda are a given. By doing this, we end the meeting death spiral—one bad meeting whose only outcome is to create another bad meeting.

SIX STEPS TO MEETINGS THAT PEOPLE ACTUALLY WANT TO BE PART OF

Your success or failure at leading a meeting starts well before you have the group in the room. The thought and planning that goes into a meeting can make or break its success. Nothing in the moment—during the meeting—can make up for lack of planning on the front end.

The six steps outlined here are not optional or nice-to-have. They are required. This is what it looks like to *treat meetings like they matter.* You need to be diligent in these steps, whether you are planning a one-hour meeting or a one-week meeting.

THE SIX STEPS:

1. Attempt to talk yourself out of it
2. Get really clear on your outcomes
3. Craft your agenda
4. Invite and prepare the right people
5. Facilitate the heck out of it
6. Follow up and hold people accountable

Done poorly, meetings can undermine every message you are trying to send about the meeting itself, as well as the project and you as the leader. Here's what can happen if you neglect any of the six steps:

IF YOU DON'T...	YOU ARE TELLING PEOPLE...
... attempt to talk yourself out of it: ▐▐▌►	*"I like to meet for the sake of meeting. I've got nothing better to do, and I assume you don't either."*
... get really clear on your outcomes: ... craft your agenda: ... invite and prepare the right people: ▐▐▌►	*"This meeting isn't important enough (and your time isn't important enough) for me to spend any time on it."*
... facilitate the heck out of it: ▐▐▌►	*"I'm not disciplined and won't hold you to that standard."*
... follow up and hold accountable: ▐▐▌►	*"What we talked about was really important at the time, but not as important once we went back to the real world"*

Not exactly the tone you want to set if you are looking to increase your influence and motivate people to support your project or decision. To make meetings matter, you need to cover all six steps.

STEP 1. ATTEMPT TO TALK YOURSELF OUT OF IT

Let's go back to Jeanine. She had some customer data that she wanted to "tell people about." Before going any further, she needs to try to talk herself out of it. Meetings should be the exception, not the rule. Not sure if you should have the meeting? Ask the people you would invite to attend. Do they think a meeting is necessary?

Some good reasons to hold a meeting include: solve a problem, brainstorm ideas, make a decision, plan/create. Some bad reasons include: discuss, explore, share information. So for Jeanine, wanting to "talk about customer data" may not be a good reason to hold a meeting, unless she can answer affirmatively to one of these questions:

Is the information urgent and they must hear it from you, either because it is sensitive or you are the only messenger who can or should deliver it? An example of this would be a major personnel announcement.

Does the message need to be delivered to a set of people at the same time for consistency of message and to prevent any "leaking" of your message? A major announcement like a project cancellation would fall into this category.

Is the information not self-explanatory, or would making it self-explanatory take more time and effort than is warranted? If Jeanine's customer information was so complex that it couldn't stand alone, she would want to hold an information-sharing meeting.

Always consider your options to a meeting—alternative forms of communication, one-to-one conversations, etc. Never assume that a meeting is the answer.

Never assume a meeting is the answer; consider your options.

MINDSET

STEP 2. GET VERY, VERY SPECIFIC ON OUTCOMES

I truly don't believe that people wake up one morning and say, "You know what, I am going to call a meeting next week that has absolutely no purpose and is a complete waste of time." I'm sure Jeanine-with-the-customer-data didn't roll out of bed thinking this way. Each meeting holds some nugget of value—an important question that needs to be answered, some problem that needs to be solved. However, many times we do a really good job of hiding it. Maybe this is because we think its value is self-evident, or we sense that there is a purpose but can't put our finger on it?

Remember Anne back in Essential #5 who was trying to influence the horrible senior leadership meetings? The General Manager had a vague sense of what he wanted to get out of the meetings, which is fine if you are having a one-hour business lunch with someone. But when you are pulling multiple people together, for a long period of time and, in this case, from around the world, you have to get specific.

Think about why you want to pull the meeting together. Write it down, don't just get a general sense of why you need to have it. Get specific and be prepared to answer the question in a sentence or two (because you will have to answer it in a sentence or two when people question the need for the meeting).

Differentiating between what I call *outcome verbs* and *talk verbs* is really important when you are thinking about a meeting's outcome. Here's the difference:

The purpose of this meeting is to...

Outcome Verbs	**Talk Verbs**
Resolve	Discuss
Decide	Explore
Identify	Share
Create	Confer

The first list lends itself to physical manifestation. This is a good bias. What will be lying on the table at the end of the meeting? An answer to a question? A decision? A plan? A list of prioritized issues? Even if it won't literally be a physical product, if you think of it this way it is easier to form your agenda and ultimately direct the conversation. Discussion, exploration and sharing may also happen, but they are not your ultimate goal.

If your goal does not fit neatly into this first list, go back to Step 1 and attempt to talk yourself out of it. There are probably other ways to make this happen, or at least ways to begin information sharing so that you can move quickly into the next phase (i.e., resolve, decide, etc.). If there isn't a next phase, you need to question why they need the information at all.

Your outcome is the starting point for your agenda. Let's go back to Jeanine and her meeting on customer data. Notice that she started with the need to "talk about the data." For Jeanine, like everyone else, talk verbs are not great when Nick Naysayer is on the invite list. When Nick calls and asks, "What is this meeting all about? Do we really need it?" and Jeanine replies with "We are going to talk about…" she makes it easy for Nick to discount the meeting (and accidently double-book himself or multi-task during the meeting). If Jeanine is able to respond with a solid meeting outcome like, *"The purpose of the meeting is to review customer data and decide what we will act on and when,"* her rationale is much more powerful, and the chance of Nick making the meeting a priority increases.

STEP 3. CRAFT YOUR AGENDA (HINT: IT IS NOT A LIST OF TOPICS)

If the #1 no-no is calling a meeting without an agenda, then the follow-up no-no is providing a lame agenda—a list of topics to cover. An agenda is much more than this. If you only have a list of topics to cover, go back to Step 1 and consider alternatives to a meeting.

Your agenda should take your participants from point A to point B to their final destination: the outcome you identified in the previous step. The agenda represents the thought process you are going to take them through to reach your endpoint. It is also a visual aid for your participants. You are most likely competing with others in the matrix for their attention, so your agenda better look like it is setting up for high-impact conversation and decision-making or it will be moved to the bottom of the priority list.

A typical outcome-focused agenda has three phases: (1) get grounded, (2) discuss and (3) land. "Get grounded" is your introduction—what you are going to accomplish, why it is important and how you are going to do it. "Discuss" is where you generate options, ideas and possibilities. Notice that "Discuss" is a talk verb. This is fine for one step in your agenda, just not as your endpoint. "Land" can represent a decision, plan, next steps—whatever your destination is.

Here's how Jeanine's meeting might look as a list of topics vs. the three phases:

LIST OF TOPICS AGENDA	STRUCTURED THOUGHT PATTERN AGENDA
Meeting Outcome: To review customer data and decide what we will act on and when	*Meeting Outcome: To review customer data and decide what we will act on and when*
9:00 – 9:15 Customer feedback on current pricing	9:00 – 9:15 Review key customer data on pricing and delivery method [Get grounded]
9:15 – 9:30 Customer feedback on new delivery method	9:15 – 9:45 Identify which issues have biggest impact on customer retention [Discuss]
9:30 – 10:00 Customer feedback on Returns policy	9:45 – 10:00 Determine next steps and owners for priority items [Land]

The agenda on the left is vague and only supports a "Talk" outcome. The agenda on the right supports Jeanine's outcome by providing steps that will guide the group's thinking from open-ended discussion to agreed-upon next steps. What's going to make this agenda really fly is Step 4: invite the right people and get them prepared.

STEP 4. INVITE THE RIGHT PEOPLE AND GET THEM PREPARED

I had a client who was becoming increasingly frustrated by the lack of progress in his meetings with a group of technical experts. They couldn't gain any traction; they couldn't reach decisions. The people in the meetings kept saying, "I'll have to get back to you." I asked him who these people went back to talk to and he identified two people—Francois and Karen. Clearly it was Francois and Karen who needed to be invited to the meetings, not these folks. Alternatively, Francois and Karen needed to deputize those attending with some decision-making authority.

Decision-makers or those they have deputized should be at the top of your invite list. Beyond these people, select wisely based on your outcome and agenda. Even in ongoing teams, there are no automatics on who to invite. Not every meeting needs to involve every person on your team. Decide who needs to be at the table and invite the appropriate people. Those without a defined purpose will distract, take up space and pull the meeting away from its intended outcome, leaving everyone feeling frustrated. This "agenda-based" participation should be transparent and, when possible, set up from the beginning of a project to prevent people from guessing or inventing why they weren't invited.

Invite lists are tricky in a matrix role because so many people are involved. A friend of mine (and customer hub matrix player) told me a great story of a customer meeting. The list of attendees started to grow because everyone in the hub thought their attendance was critical. They showed up at the customer site, and the customer didn't have a conference room big enough so half of them had to wait in the lobby.

As this story illustrates, there is great risk of over-including in matrix roles. Strive to be inclusive but not all-inclusive. This is where having a clear outcome is critical, as is role clarity (Essential #3). Without these, narrowing the invite list becomes almost impossible. When you narrow, make sure you are transparent about it.

When considering your invite list, give it a litmus test. For each person, list why they must be there and what you expect them to do both in the meeting and as a result of the meeting. If there are a lot of "know," "understand" or "be aware of" statements, question whether they need to be there. These are the invite equivalents of talk verbs—"know verbs" that tell you a person needs to be informed, but not in attendance. There are a lot of ways to inform; meeting attendance is not required.

If you are being selective on whom to invite, make sure key people will be in attendance. If you call a meeting when you know key people can't come, you'll basically spend the meeting talking about what you wanted to talk about in the meeting—dancing around the topic, "Well, we'll have to wait to see what Jim has to say before we can move forward on this." Decisions get deferred, more meetings are scheduled and you have to spend time bringing the absent people up to speed. Arrange the meeting for a time when you know key people can be there.

Once you get the invite list nailed down, think about how to make sure attendees are ready to hit the ground running at minute one of the meeting. Rarely do you want a group to walk in completely flat-footed, but you don't have to ask them to prepare 50 slides either. Give them something to do ahead of time, and don't just ask them to "think about something." Ask them to bring something in—again think "physical," just like your outcome statement. Here are a few examples:

> » Review and note which alternative...
> » Identify three priorities...
> » Bring in three concerns your team has...

This constitutes your pre-work and serves a specific purpose; it is not just a "nice to have." People don't do pre-work because they can slide by without it—they are busy, and this is one thing they can get away with not doing. Make it clear how you will use the pre-work and why it is imperative to do it. Let them know that you will be asking for this information in your cover note or in the pre-work itself, something like "I will ask each of you what you came in with..."

You can also build your pre-work into your agenda so they see how it is going to be used. Here's what Jeanine's agenda might look like with the pre-work embedded:

Meeting Outcome:
To review customer data and decide what we will act on and when

9:00 – 9:15: Review key customer data on pricing, delivery method
[PRE-WORK: Please review attached Customer Visit Summary]

9:15 – 9:45: Identify which issues have biggest impact on customer retention
[PRE-WORK: Indicate your top three issues on the Customer Visit Summary]

9:45 – 10:00: Determine next steps and owners for priority items
[PRE-WORK: Identify people from your team who could play a role in resolution of your top three issues]

She is giving them very specific instructions for their pre-work. It is not just something they need to review (and that they can easily skip). It is clear that they are actually going to talk about it—in other words be held accountable for the pre-work.

Don't be afraid to postpone a meeting if you walk in and find that people haven't done their homework. Set a precedent that when you include pre-work, it is required and adds value to the meeting. It isn't busy work. It usually only takes one cancellation to shift a group's behavior.

Lastly, give adequate notice whenever possible. Many people prefer to think things through ahead of time rather than speak off the cuff. Attendees who are highly organized will participate much more vigorously if they are given adequate time to prepare for the meeting. Show your discipline in planning and give user-friendly, realistic pre-work, and they will be fully engaged and ready to work, not wondering why they are there and what they are supposed to accomplish.

STEP 5: FACILITATE THE HECK OUT OF IT

Have you ever participated in an elegantly facilitated meeting like Pete's meeting that I described in the introduction? It is a thing of beauty. People conflict but are heard and respected, and in the end they land on something. They walk away from the meeting feeling as if their time made a difference. Often such a meeting is the one thing they remember about the day as they drive home—there's a spot in my day that I accomplished something.

If you are wondering if you have ever facilitated such a meeting, I would ask you, have people ever gushed over one of your meetings? I find people make a point to tell you when it was a great, productive meeting. They spontaneously appreciate the fact that you gave everything you could so that their time was not wasted. They are grateful that yours was an island in a sea of crappy meetings.

So if people aren't gushing, you probably aren't facilitating, or at least not facilitating effectively. Another sign of good facilitation is exhaustion. If you don't walk away from facilitating a meeting feeling worn out, you probably aren't facilitating. When you facilitate, you do more than introduce the topics, watch the time and call the meeting to a close. You have to listen, connect all comments and stay several steps ahead to see where the conversation is going and determine whether you will need to redirect. Your mind never wanders: you are 100% attentive, 100% of the time.

It isn't easy, but people appreciate good facilitation so much because they feel like you just took their time and ideas and helped them mold it into something meaningful. A good facilitator can make even modest progress seem huge.

Facilitation is a skill that matrix managers use in almost every conversation they have. If you are the traffic cop or connector between two sides of the matrix, you are constantly bringing people and ideas together. Meetings just happen to be the formal, public version of this.

FACILITATOR ROLES. Facilitation is a complex skill best learned by watching others. Don't have any skilled facilitators around? The good news is you can learn from non-examples as well. And there are plenty of poor facilitators out there!

Here are the key roles that a facilitator plays. Every group and every topic will require a different combination and proportion of these roles.

» Keep focus
» Connect ideas
» Balance participation
» Keep things moving toward desired outcome
» Manage time

KEEP FOCUS. I remember a small group of senior folks that I was attempting to facilitate early in my career. For many different reasons, their meetings were a train wreck. At one point, I literally stood on a chair waving my hands in an attempt to get them back on track. Keeping focus is arguably the most challenging of facilitator roles. Tangents, side conversations and personal conflicts lurk around every corner. The good news is that there is more at your disposal than standing on a chair like a mad woman.

First and foremost, you need to keep the meeting's outcome at the forefront. You can do this by posting your outcome somewhere everyone can see like the wall or top of the agenda. Introduce each part of the meeting by stating the goal for that issue and describing the process you plan to use. This helps everyone focus on the same task.

Keep the conversation focused by referring back to the objective and agenda.

ZOOM OUT

You can also keep things on track by referring to the agenda, *"That's a great point, we will get to that a little later in the agenda—write it down and remind me if I don't bring it up when we get there."* Or, if it doesn't fall within the parameters of your agenda, use a "parking lot" to capture important topics that should be discussed at another time. If you commit to discussing a topic later in the meeting or put it in a Parking Lot, be sure you actually go back to it. If the topic is outside the meeting's scope, say so. Don't create the illusion that it is something to be addressed.

Finally, you will need to keep the individual energy and attention focused on the task, not extra-curricular interpersonal issues. Conflicts come up in group settings, and whether it is a personal attack on you or someone else, as the facilitator you need to respond to it.

Your first response to a disruptive comment or behavior should be subtle. Reframe the comment in a positive way. If Kim, a participant in Jeanine's customer data meeting, gets fired up and says, "Roger, it's no wonder the customer reacted that way. You and your team have been completely negligent on this for months," attempt to restate her criticism, minus the emotion: "OK, Kim, you think the customer reaction can be tracked back to some negligence on our part. Where do you think we are falling short?" Take the finger-pointing out of it and don't match the tone. If you are Kim's target, pause for a minute. You will be surprised how many times the group jumps in for you. Don't rush to defend. As a facilitator, you don't want to be seen as leveraging the position to defend yourself. If you pause and no one jumps in, reframe it much the way you would if it was directed toward someone else.

When responding to a disruptive comment, stay neutral. Restate the information, minus the tone.

JUJITSU

If the subtle approach doesn't work, be more direct. Don't match their tone, but address the tone. So, if Kim doesn't respond to the subtle approach and keeps attacking Roger or you, say something like, "Kim, this is the second time you've brought this up today, and it is obvious you are pretty frustrated. If this is something you need to talk to Roger about offline, then that is great, but right now we need to channel some of that energy toward the solution." You can use the same approach if you are in the cross-hairs: acknowledge the emotion, suggest talking about it outside the meeting and ask to channel comments toward the solution.

When you have to address a negative behavior, remember that while the offender may be a bit chastised, everyone else in the meeting will inwardly be applauding you. Also keep in mind that often your role as facilitator gives your comments extra weight. You probably will not need to come down too hard—just acknowledging the behavior is more than is usually done, and usually enough to get someone to back off. You also need to tread lightly because chances are if this person is in a meeting with you they are an ongoing part of your matrix, and the relationship needs to be preserved.

CONNECT IDEAS. A facilitator colleague of mine calls this "stopping the plopping." Left to their own devices, groups can throw out comments, ideas and opinions randomly, without connecting or building on each other's thoughts. When they start to "plop," what you get in the end is a "pile of plop" (her words, not mine) in the middle of the table, but no synthesized pool of thought. It's OK for rapid fire brainstorming, but as an ongoing meeting practice, it is not constructive.

When you connect ideas, you are comparing or combining comments. Doing this helps manage and mold the pile on the table. It shows progress toward the goal, highlights common ground and gradually builds toward a shared idea. Here are some examples of statements that manage the plop:

> *"That's sounds similar to what Julietta said [specific comment]—is that fair to say?"*

> *"So compare that to what Wayne mentioned earlier about [specific comment]—is this an example of what he had proposed?*

> *"I've heard several people mention issues around [specific topic]—do we have some agreement that this might be an area of focus?"*

Notice that all of these connections are tentative, and you are asking for verification. Verifying the connection makes sure that you have heard correctly, and it shows people that you expect them to listen and build on each other's ideas. Often after a few prompts from you, they will start their own connecting.

State your connections tentatively; ask for verification.

JUJITSU

BALANCE PARTICIPATION. Getting talkative people to pull back or quiet people to speak up is a challenge. Some people talk to be heard or think out loud and end up repeating themselves or others. Others only speak up if they are committed to what they are going to say. You invited people to the meeting to hear all perspectives, not just a handful, so you need to work to balance the participation.

Here are a few ways to help your more outgoing participants take a step back and let others into the conversation:

> *"Ok, so tell me how your comment compares to Paula's— are you agreeing with what Paula said or is there a difference in there we should hear?"* (makes it clear that there is no need to repeat what others are saying just to have something to say and makes it clear that you better listen to what others are saying—not just throw stuff out).

> *"OK, let's hear from a few others."*

"We heard from Connie and Carlos, what are some other perspectives that don't fall into these two points of view?"

To get the quieter folks to speak up, try throwing out a question and then going around the table. Non-verbally encourage them to speak up by leaning forward, making eye contact and nodding. Look for subtle signs that they have something to say—a quick hand up, vigorous nodding or prolonged eye contact with you may all be signs they are ready to speak up.

Sometimes it is not personal preference that holds people back, it's the topic. When a topic becomes dominated by just two or three people and the rest are shutting off, it may be that the topic or the level of detail is not applicable to everyone. Encourage the interested parties to take it offline: "It sounds like those are some pretty specific tactics for the two of you to work out—why don't you take that offline, and we will pull things back to the bigger picture for this meeting."

KEEP THINGS MOVING. The best way to keep things moving toward your outcome is to continually tell people where you are vis-à-vis your outcome. Progress breeds progress, which in turn leads to satisfaction with the meeting and the overall process/project. It keeps people engaged and hopeful. After completing a major part of the meeting, summarize

Keep the energy of the group alive by stepping back to see progress toward the goal.

ZOOM OUT

what the group accomplished. This is one of the reasons that Pete's meetings were so motivating. When he summarized, he was celebrating the achievement, reminding everyone what they finished and formally ending the discussion.

Show bigger-picture progress too, by beginning your meetings with what was accomplished since the last meeting. "Last time we talked about x, and here's how it has been implemented." If you don't want people to feel like meetings are pointless, you have to offer some proof that they're not.

Synthesizing ideas and comments shows progress too. After a period of time generating ideas, synthesize what you have heard: "So it sounds like our options fall into four categories [list them out, ideally on a flipchart or screen]. Am I missing any?" This tightens up the discussion and moves things toward the next phase.

You will also have to help the group move forward when they become stuck. When this happens, start by labeling it and then summarize where you are and where you need to go: "It sounds like we are a little stuck. So far I have heard us identify three possible solutions, but we need to land on one to proceed with…" If that nudge doesn't move them, try to help them figure out what might get them unstuck. It may be more information, bringing another person into the discussion or just walking away for a bit. Don't let the wheels spin. Help them stay in the conversation by figuring out a way to get unstuck.

MANAGING TIME. A facilitator, while not a time-keeper (if you need one of those, delegate the task), needs to help the group be mindful of time. A good agenda helps here. Reminders and time checks like these help keep things moving: "You'll see on the agenda we have just 15 minutes to discuss this, so we will need to stay focused and on topic." "We've got about 5 minutes left on this part of the agenda, let's take one last thought and then wrap things up."

You will also need to help manage time when the group has taken a detour and that detour is impacting the timing of the meeting. If it is a positive detour, renegotiate the time parameters: "We are set to spend just five more minutes on this—but it seems like we are covering good ground—everyone OK if we either stay on an extra five minutes or take five minutes from the next agenda item?" When the detour does not appear to add value, note it and ask them to move on. What you must do is avoid unconscious departure from the agenda: you don't want to wander.

Time management starts with beginning the meeting on time. Don't recap for late people. Doing so legitimizes lateness and disrespects those who made an effort to show up on time. Also make sure you end on time. If you must run over, check in with the group. Repeatedly running over should tell you something—your agenda is too ambitious or your facilitation needs to be tighter. Finally, never be afraid to end a meeting early. A meeting that accomplishes its objective in less than the allotted time is a victory, and you are the hero.

The tone for all of these facilitator roles is pragmatic and no-nonsense. Not school marm, you are not there to shame into compliance. Setting up ground rules at the beginning of the meeting can help here. Ground rules set expectations and can serve as a starting point for correcting behavior. "We agreed to make sure that everyone was heard today, and I don't think we have heard Colleen's opinion on this yet." Ground rules can be set around level of participation, use of technology/multi-tasking, confidentiality or problem (vs. personal) focus.

A bit of self-deprecating humor also helps diffuse many situations and can help maintain relationships and participation of the group, "OK, I will play the bad cop here and say that we are breaking a few ground rules." "I don't know about you, but I feel like we have gotten lost—let me attempt to find us again."

Finally, your role as facilitator does not include filling the silence with comments. Allow silence, it gives people time to think and absorb. If you need to, check in on the silence: "So, help me read the silence—are we lost or just thinking?"

For really sticky situations a professional may be needed. But don't become over-reliant on third parties to lead your meetings. For teams that are longer-term, facilitation should be a group skill, one that everyone gets good at. A great way to do this is through training, but also consider having a professional facilitator come in for a short period of time to demonstrate the right behavior and build good habits in the team, then send them off to facilitate on their own.

STEP 6. FOLLOW UP AND HOLD ACCOUNTABLE

Your responsibilities as the meeting facilitator don't end with the close of the meeting. Following up on commitments and holding participants accountable sets the next meeting up for success—they make your meeting serious business. Often we fail to manage this "white space" and rely entirely on meetings to stand on their own. In established teams with a strong sense of accountability and a consistent meeting process, the meetings may not need follow-up. For all others, follow-up is required.

Follow-up starts with having good notes on the meeting. I hesitate to call them "minutes" because this label connotes verbatim transcription. Notes should really be a summary of who was there, what was decided, what the next steps are and who owns those next steps. Make them easy to read, with "Decisions Made" clearly marked, as well as "Next Steps." Then share them with participants and key stakeholders. "I shared our follow-ups with [a common boss, project sponsor], and she thinks they make a ton of sense."

But depending on the length of time between meetings and the maturity of your meeting process, the documentation might not be enough. If this is the case, follow-up to the group or specific individuals will ensure that your next meeting is structured appropriately (based on actual progress) and doesn't start right back from square one. This "white space" management keeps the momentum going and provides continuity for your next meeting. As mentioned in Essential #4, without follow-up the space between meetings is where decisions die. The same is true of ideas and to-do's: they can easily fade to black in the white space.

WHEN YOU AREN'T LEADING THE MEETING

Realistically, there will be plenty of meetings in your matrix that you participate in, versus lead. When you aren't leading the meeting or the project, trying to get others to adopt the principles in this chapter can be tricky. Here are a few subtle ways to shift other people's meeting behavior:

Guilt. Be the best meeting attendee ever. Ask questions, connect what people are saying, redirect conversation. Be on time. Be disciplined. Guilt everyone else into behaving better.

Volunteer. Ask the meeting leader if they want your help in agenda planning. They may view this as a welcome relief.

Demonstrate. Informally facilitate during the meeting—ask opinions, link, contrast and compare comments.

Coax. Ask questions to push a meeting leader to be more deliberate in thinking through the meeting: "What results do you think we want from the meeting? I'd like to show up prepared." "How will we choose which plan to use? I'd like to think through options ahead of time." These are questions the leader should be considering, and knowing you are one step ahead of them may push them to think things through.

Be direct. The direct approach can also be used—just frame it in a way that is all about making everyone's lives easier and advancing the project: "I noticed that we tend to spin our wheels in the first part of our meetings. I am wondering if an agenda and some pre-work might help us hit the ground running and get us to resolutions faster."

All the talk in these matrix roles is not cheap, but we treat it like it is. Rarely do we treat meetings with the reverence they deserve—you are bringing together (live or on the phone) your matrix. This is it—a test for you as a matrix master and an opportunity to do what the matrix is intended to do—bring together multiple parts of the business to solve problems that can't be solved in a vacuum.

Invest by deliberately planning and tactfully facilitating your meetings. They won't all be perfect—they may even get worse before they get better as you try out some of these approaches. Learn from these bad experiences, as well as the meetings that people say positive things about. If someone says it was a great meeting, ask him or her what made it good.

Good meeting facilitation is not common practice. Few people have the skills, and most of us sit through poorly run meetings, develop a lot of bad habits and then, when it's our turn to step up and lead, just don't have the skills to do it. Become an observer. Some of the best facilitation techniques are very, very subtle. Notice what effective facilitators say and do to move a group forward. Take these approaches and blend them with your own style of expressing things for really powerful facilitation that you will use daily in your matrix role—in meetings and out.

IN SUMMARY

EMBRACE

→ Meetings matter. They are not a departure from work; in a matrix they are your work, and you get out of them what you put into them.

→ A structured, discipline approach to planning them, which starts with a clear outcome.

→ Your role as an active facilitator. There is not a role you can play that will be as appreciated as much as this is. People are grateful for those who don't waste their time and help them create something they couldn't on their own.

→ Your role in managing the "white space" between meetings—don't let the matrix drown out all the work that was done and assigned in your meeting. Follow up and keep it alive.

→ Your role as a meeting participant. Even if you aren't leading the meeting, there are safe, subtle ways to make it better.

TRY

→ Give your meeting outcome the "on the table" test. Ask yourself what you want to be sitting in the middle of the table at the end of the meeting. This will help you structure your agenda and facilitate effectively.

→ Check your agenda; make sure it reflects a thought process, not a list of topics

→ Keep the purpose of the meeting visible—it helps keep conversation on track and can keep people motivated toward the accomplishment

→ As the leader, keep track of the follow-up nudges you will need to provide in the white space so that decisions and tasks don't get lost between meetings

IN PRACTICE

The mindset and strategies outlined in this chapter hold true regardless of the type of matrix you are in—unlike the other Essentials, there are no specific tips or nuances that are specific to role type. Meetings are where the parts of any matrix come together and either collide or converge. No matter where you are in any type of matrix, your ability to succeed at meetings will lead to greater success in all your other endeavors.

PUTTING IT ALL TOGETHER

So you have finished the book, now what?

Here are a few things to consider:

→ It starts with you. Just like the principle we talked about in Essential #1, it starts with you and you should keep on doing it even when no one else is following suit. Don't wait for the organization to improve its matrix, improve your own.

→ Don't rely on one essential for your success, you will need more than that for sustained achievement. Make it your goal to improve in other areas, don't just continue to leverage one strength.

→ The seven essentials work in concert. Don't try to find one panacea. If you or your team is struggling, look at multiple diagnoses and solutions.

→ Change the conversation. Too much of our talk about the matrix revolves around complaints and criticism. This book provides a framework and language for discussing the matrix constructively. Whether it is discussing man-made versus natural goal misalignments or role clarity versus role acceptance, this book provides a frame for discussing issues in an objective way.

PUTTING IT ALL TOGETHER

→ Keep learning. Here are a few of the resources I mentioned in the book (and a few others that I turn to often) that will help you in your journey:

» *The Seven Habits of Highly Effective People*
Stephen R. Covey

» *Crucial Conversations and Crucial Confrontations*
Patterson et al. 2002, 2005

» *The Triangle of Truth*
Lisa Earle McLeod, 2010

» *Getting Together As We Negotiate*
Fisher and Brown, 1988

» *The Trusted Advisor*
Maister et al. 2000

» *Decision Traps: The Ten Barriers to Brillant Decision-making and How to Overcome Them*
Russo and Schoemaker, 1989

» *Power, Influence and Persuasion*
Harvard Business Essentials, 2005

Keep in touch!
Connect with other matrix practitioners on
www.masterthematrixblog.com!

ACKNOWLEGEMENTS

For me this book was personal. I spent my first 12 months in my first matrix role driving into work hoping the building had burned down. After being successful in a small organization where I knew how to get things done, it was like the earth had tilted on its axis. I was out of sync with everything and everyone around me.

But writing was also a social endeavor. "It takes a village," is one of my favorite sayings. This book took a village, or more appropriately, a matrix.

To my family who put up with me during "The Year of the Book," "thanks" is not a strong enough word. My husband Patrick kept everything else moving while I was holed up in my office at the keyboard or on the phone. Only once did he recommend that I perhaps give up the writing and stick to things I knew I was good at. He was my first reader and patiently listened as I dissected every chapter on our evening walks.

My children, each in their own unique way, encouraged me. Meg, an aspiring author herself, motivated me to prove that it could be done. And in a move uncharacteristic of her tween status, told me how very cool she thought it was. Abby's frequent and sincere questions of "How'd you do on your book today, Mommy?" always made me smile and keep me going. Sean motivated me by challenging me to sell more than his estimated seven books ("Seriously, Mom, who's going to buy a book about a matrix?")

My professional help included Wally Bock, a writing coach who never ceased to inform, challenge and be my cheerleader. Each time I concluded a conversation with him I felt like I could take on the world. Kevin Fitzgerald was my book designer extraordinaire. I know him because he is family, I picked him because he is uber-talented. Emilie Moore is the editor everyone needs to have—as dedicated to the book as I was, she performed superhuman feats to make this happen. My friend and writing partner Paula Kluth can be blamed for setting me on this journey. Kathy Kowalczyk, my virtual assistant, kept me organized and on top of all the details (which isn't easy). Many, many thanks to all of you.

A special thanks goes to Harry Kraemer for authoring the foreword. So much of what I appreciate and know about matrix roles is due to his leadership at Baxter. He is one of the original matrix masters.

Over 100 people were gracious enough to participate in the survey that was the start of this research. To those mostly nameless folks, thank you for your perspective. The following people took time to meet with me to share their stories and ideas—I hope the book does them justice:

Lynne Andia
Robert Axelrod
K.V. Balachander
Cindy Bellek
Karen Blair
Mike Blume
Paul Brenner
Ila Brouder
Kathy Buscaglia
Jim Carne
Scott Cleve
Jim Cronin
Len Czuba
Joe Duffy
Tim Finnigan
Kathleen S. Fliss
Steve Garchow
Lee Guthman

Ron Healy
Carolyn Henning
Mary Hoffman
Janice Howse
Kyle Johnson
Brian Kenney
Ed Lamb
Lisa Leigeber
Griff Lewis
Jennifer Lueck
Kary M. Mason
Jeanne McWhorter
Dan M. Mihai
Mike Minarich
Terry Newman
Constance Nichols, MD
Tara Nofziger
David Pidduck

Brian Piper, PMP
Jim Plewa
Randy Rice
Sangita Richardson
Mark Rimbergas
Mike Rittenhouse
Al Ritter
Maximo Neira Schliemann
Jennifer Schmidt
Janet Rowland Siladi
Nina Simosko
Michelle Smith
Angela Stauder
Mary Stern
Padma Taggarse
Sara Tripp, MS, PMP
Lauren White
Kathy Young

Last but not least all the clients, colleagues and friends who encouraged me. Thanks so much for your interest, stories and support, especially those times when you urged me on with your most recent matrix frustration with appeals for me to "write faster!" You helped me on my journey; I hope this book helps you on yours.

ABOUT THE AUTHOR

Susan Finerty has been working in matrix roles and with matrix organizations for more than 20 years. Since 2004, she has developed a consulting practice focused on organizational effectiveness—helping organizations design and implement change, helping teams work effectively together and coaching individuals on communication, influence and leadership. She has held adjunct faculty roles at Northwestern University and Loyola University-Chicago. She has a blog focused on leadership that can be found at www.LeadershipMutt.com and a blog focused on matrix management at www.masterthematrixblog.com. She holds a BA from Central Michigan University and an MA from Indiana University. She resides in suburban Chicago with her husband and three children.

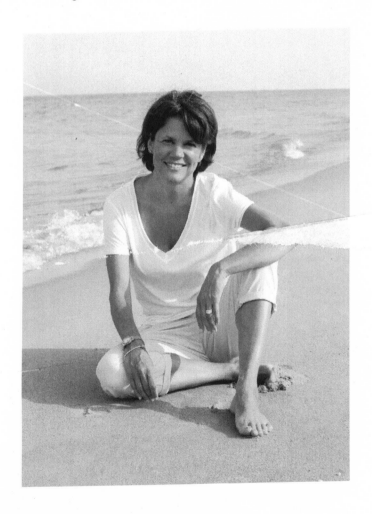